TEACHING CHILDREN WITH
AUTISM TO MIND-READ

TEACHING CHILDREN WITH AUTISM TO MIND-READ

A Practical Guide
for Teachers and Parents

Patricia Howlin
St George's Hospital Medical School
University of London

Simon Baron-Cohen
University of Cambridge

Julie Hadwin
University of Kent

JOHN WILEY & SONS
Chichester · New York · Weinheim · Brisbane · Singapore · Toronto

Copyright © 1999   John Wiley & Sons Ltd, The Atrium, Southern Gate, Chichester,
West Sussex PO19 8SQ, England

Telephone   (+44) 1243 779777

Email (for orders and customer service enquiries): cs-books@wiley.co.uk
Visit our Home Page on www.wileyeurope.com or www.wiley.com

Reprinted March and December 1999, November 2000, January and December 2002, October 2003,
February 2005, April and November 2006, July and December 2007, September 2008

This publication is designed to provide accurate and authoritative information in regard to
the subject matter covered. It is sold on the understanding that the Publisher is not engaged in
rendering professional services. If professional advice or other expert assistance is required,
the services of a competent professional should be sought.

Other Wiley Editorial Offices

John Wiley & Sons Inc., 111 River Street, Hoboken, NJ 07030, USA

Jossey-Bass, 989 Market Street, San Francisco, CA 94103-1741, USA

Wiley-VCH Verlag GmbH, Boschstr. 12, D-69469 Weinheim, Germany

John Wiley & Sons Australia Ltd, 33 Park Road, Milton, Queensland 4064, Australia

John Wiley & Sons (Asia) Pte Ltd, 2 Clementi Loop #02-01, Jin Xing Distripark, Singapore
129809

John Wiley & Sons Canada Ltd, 22 Worcester Road, Etobicoke, Ontario, Canada M9W 1L1

British Library Cataloguing in Publication Data

A catalogue record for this book is available from the British Library

ISBN-13: 978-0-471-97623-3 (P/B)

Typeset in 11/13pt Times by Wyvern 21 Ltd, Bristol
Printed and bound in Great Britain by CPI Antony Rowe, Chippenham, Wiltshire

Contents

List of Figures

List of Tables

A note to teachers and parents

You will find a wealth of pictorial material in this Guide for your practical use at home or in the classroom. Don't be put off by the quantity of material. It has been included to enable you to work through many examples in subtly different ways, to enhance your child's understanding of the mind, thoughts, intentions, desires, and emotions. At times you may also wonder at the technical terms used (e.g. in the Introduction). Again, do not be deterred, since these are included simply so as to provide all the scientific background for the professional reader. We hope the Guide will be self-explanatory, through the pictures, and that you find it of value. We, the authors, would be delighted to hear from you as to how you find using it.

Acknowledgements

This work was funded as project grants to Simon Baron-Cohen and Pat Howlin by the Mental Health Foundation and Bethlem-Maudsley Trust. It was published as:

Hadwin, J., Baron-Cohen, S., Howlin, P., & Hill, K., (1996) Can we teach children with autism to understand emotions, belief, or pretence? *Development and Psychopathology*. **8**, 345–365.

Part I
Introduction

BACKGROUND AND AIMS
OF THE GUIDE

Autism is a complex disorder that affects many aspects of a child's functioning. Social and communicative development are particularly disrupted, even in individuals who are of normal non-verbal intelligence, and these difficulties are exacerbated by rigid behaviour patterns, obsessional interests and routines.[1] Although the "enigma" of autism[2] has inspired an enormous amount of research the causes of the condition remain poorly understood. Genetic factors are clearly important in many cases, although at the time of writing no specific genetic mechanism has been found. Effective treatments, usually of a behavioural nature, can be used to reduce some of the secondary problems associated with autism[3] but social and communicative abnormalities tend to prove more resistant to intervention. It is on the remediation of such problems that this Guide concentrates.

PREVIOUS ATTEMPTS TO
IMPROVE SOCIAL AND COMMUNICATIVE
DEFICITS IN AUTISM

There are literally hundreds of studies that claim to enhance the social and communication skills of children and adults with autism.[4] Drug, vitamin and dietary treatments, interventions based on "holding", "music" or "pet" therapies, facilitated communication, sensory and physical stimulation programmes, and many others, all have their advocates. Unfortunately, the claims for success are rarely supported by experimental evidence. The interventions that have proved most successful are those involving a high degree of structure, with a focus on the development of more appropriate social and communication skills.[5] The use of non-disabled peers as therapists has been explored in a number of studies[6] and techniques to reduce anxiety have also been found to be effective in improving social interactions.[7] Role-play and drama techniques, too, can be used to develop social skills, whilst video recordings can be useful for providing feed-back and helping to reduce obviously abnormal behaviours such as inappropriate eye gaze, facial grimacing, or odd vocalisations.[8]

LIMITATIONS OF TRADITIONAL APPROACHES TO INTERVENTION

Although communication and social skills programmes can have an important impact on some aspects of social functioning, generalisation to untrained settings is frequently limited. Moreover, there is often little evidence of more general improvements in social *understanding*. The synchronisation of verbal and non-verbal skills (such as eye-contact, smiles and gestures) also remains poor.[9] Since problems in social understanding are so fundamental to autism it is perhaps hardly surprising that intervention programmes that concentrate on *specific* impairments have only limited success. It seems reasonable to assume, therefore, that a focus on developing key aspects of social understanding could result in more widespread changes in social behaviour. That is, rather than attempting to change specific behaviours in specific situations, interventions aimed at improving social understanding might produce wider, *qualitative* changes in individuals' social and communication skills.

What, however, are the key aspects of social understanding that are most likely to have such an impact on overall development? Recent studies of young, normal children have stressed the importance of the development of a "theory of mind", and it is around this area that we suggest future intervention programmes need to place particular emphasis.

THE NORMAL CHILD AS A MIND-READER[10]

A "theory of mind" is defined as the ability to infer other people's mental states (their thoughts, beliefs, desires, intentions, etc), and the ability to use this information to interpret what they say, make sense of their behaviour and predict what they will do next. By the time toddlers start to speak it is clear that they talk about actions in terms of mental states. From as early as 18–30 months, normal children refer to a range of mental states: emotions, desires, beliefs, thoughts, dreams, pretence, etc.[11,12] By the age of 3–4 years, as experimental studies show, the child's theory of mind is well developed. Recent debates have, however, questioned whether this type of understanding is properly called a "theory". We do not discuss this issue here, but instead use the more neutral term of "mind-reading".

Dennett[13] proposed that the "acid test" of whether a child is able to mind-read arises in situations involving *false belief*. Thus, if the child knows the money is in the old china vase, but that Burglar Bill *thinks* it's in the desk drawer, if asked where Burglar Bill will look for the money the child should judge that he will look in the *wrong* place — the desk drawer. Using a false belief task, Wimmer and Perner[14] showed that children of around 4 years of age were able to pass such a test. An adaptation of their procedure[15] is illustrated in Figure 1.1.

As can be seen, the test involves appreciating that since Sally was absent when her marble was moved from its original location, she didn't *see* it being moved and so she won't *know* it was moved, and therefore must still *believe* it is in its original position. When asked: "Where will Sally look for her marble?" (i.e. a Belief Question) the vast majority of 4 year old children are able to answer correctly.

The ability to understand false beliefs is a complex one, because the child has to take into account Sally's belief in order to make the correct prediction about her behaviour. However, even at a much earlier stage normal children appear to be well aware that people have information in their heads – that is that they have informational states. An early sign of such understanding is seen in their ability to pass tests of visual perspective-taking. Two levels of visual perspective-taking can be identified. The first is called Level 1 — the ability to infer *what* another person can see. This appears to be present even by 2 years of age.[16] Thus, 2 year olds can put things out of or bring things into sight, when requested to do so. Level 2 visual perspective-taking is the ability to infer *how* the object appears to another person. This seems to take longer to develop. In fact it is not until 3–4 years of age that children reliably pass Level 2 tasks. For example, when shown a picture of a turtle which appears either right-side up or upside-down (depending on which side of the table it is viewed from), young 3 year olds fail to identify correctly which of these two perspectives the experimenter would have, when his or her perspective differs from that of the child.

A related achievement in the development of mind-reading is in children's understanding of the principle that "seeing-leads-to-knowing". For example, 3 year olds are easily able to indicate which of two people will *know* what is in a container, if one of them has *looked* into the container whilst the other has simply touched it.[17] Such an ability demonstrates that even at this young age, children are aware of the importance of *access to information* in acquiring knowledge.

So much for tests of children's understanding of informational states. What about their understanding of desire and emotion? Desire is often thought to be *the* other key mental state, next to belief, in understanding others' behaviour. With beliefs and desires, all kinds of behaviour become interpretable. For example, in watching a movie and trying to understand why the protagonist tiptoes into his empty flat, we

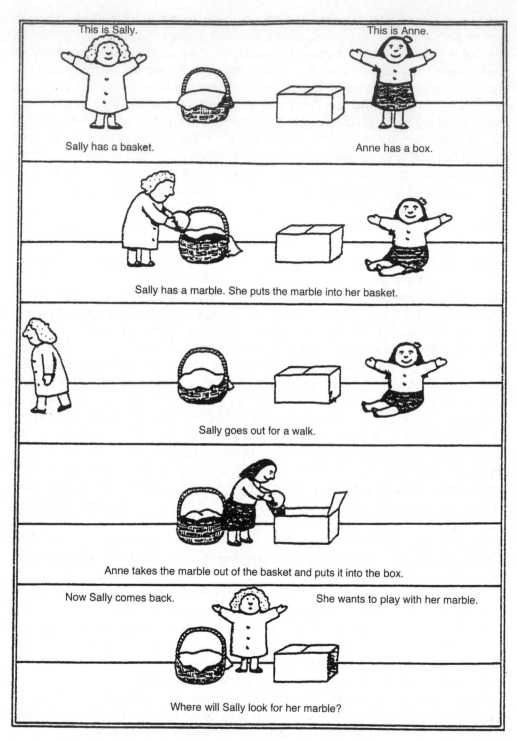

Figure 1.1 The Sally Anne scenario (reproduced from Baron-Cohen, Leslie and Frith, 1985; with kind permission).

might refer to his *belief* that there is someone in the flat and his *desire* to get in unnoticed. Several studies show that for normal children, desire is understood earlier than belief — in fact, desire is clearly understood by normal two year olds.[18] Indeed, the "terrible twos" have been interpreted as evidence of this age group's growing awareness of the frustrating difference between their own and their parents' desires.

With regard to the understanding of emotion, even young infants can discriminate facial expressions of happy, sad, angry and afraid. By 3 years old they can predict how situations affect emotions and by the age of 4 they can take into account both someone's desires *and* beliefs in predicting how they will feel. For example, if John *wants* a new book but *thinks* that something else is inside the package he will *feel* sad.

Another important mental state that has been well studied is that of pretence. Children begin to produce pretend play from as early as 10–18 months of age.[19] Experiments with verbal children also show that as soon as they can answer questions, they seem to understand that pretence is distinct from reality.[20] Thus, although they may play with a banana *as if it were* a telephone, they have no difficulty in recognising the real function of both objects. This is clearly a complex achievement.

THE IMPORTANCE OF MIND-READING: WHAT DO WE USE IT FOR?

Making sense of social behaviour

At this stage, it is worth pausing to reflect on *why* children are acquiring this extraordinarily rich body of knowledge: what are the benefits to the child in being able to mind read? Dennett was perhaps one of the first to put forward the case for the necessary role of mind-reading in understanding the human world. Attributing mental states to people is by far the easiest way of understanding them. By understanding, Dennett meant formulating explanations of their behaviour and predicting what they would do next.

Mind-reading also goes under the name of "folk psychology", and this may be a better term for it. The attraction of talking about this ability in terms of folk psychology is that it reminds us that it is simply our everyday way of understanding people. As Dennett points out:

> We use folk psychology all the time, to explain and predict each other's behaviour; we attribute beliefs and desires to each other with confidence — and quite unselfconsciously — and spend a substantial portion of our waking lives formulating the world — not excluding ourselves — in these terms . . .

Every time we venture out on the highway, for example, we stake our lives on the reliability of our general expectations about the perceptual beliefs, normal desires and decision proclivities of the other motorists. We find . . . that it is a theory of great generative power and efficiency. For instance, watching a film with a highly original and unstereotyped plot, we see the hero smile at the villain and we all swiftly and effortlessly arrive at the same complex theoretical diagnosis: 'Aha!' we conclude (but perhaps not consciously), 'He wants her to think that he doesn't know she intends to defraud her brother!'[21]

Making sense of communication

A second function of mind-reading is in understanding communication. Perhaps the clearest case for this was put by Grice,[22] a philosopher of language. He argued that the key thing that we do when we search for meaning in what someone has said, is to imagine what their *communicative intention* might be. So, when the cop shouts "Drop it!", the robber is not left in a state of acute doubt over the ambiguity of the term "it". Rather, the robber makes a rapid assumption that the cop *intended* to use the word "it" to refer to the gun in the robber's hand, and furthermore *intended* the robber to recognize his *intention* to use the word in this way. Similarly, if the art teacher instructs her pupils: "Today we're all going to paint the rabbit in his cage", everyone in the class is aware that this does not mean that the unfortunate rabbit should be covered with paint. Clearly, in decoding *figurative* speech (such as irony, sarcasm, metaphor, or humour), the ability to mind-read is essential, since in such cases the speaker does not *intend* his or her words to be taken literally.

This analysis of language in terms of complex communicative intentions makes clear that in decoding speech we are doing a lot more than simply working through the spoken words. We are going beyond what we hear, to hypothesize about the speaker's mental state. Grice did not limit this analysis to speech but argued that exactly the same process was used in non-verbal communication. Thus, if Individual A gestures towards the doorway with an outstretched arm and with the palm of the hand open, Individual B would immediately assume that A means (= *intends* B to *understand*) that he should go through the doorway.

The other way in which mind-reading is held to play an essential part in successful communication is in the speaker monitoring his or her listener's *informational needs*: that is, in judging what the listener already *knows* or does not know, and what information must still be supplied in order that the listener can *understand* the communicative intention. Furthermore, for communication to succeed, the speaker needs to be monitoring whether their message has been *understood* as they intended it to be, or if rephrasing is required to clarify ambiguity. Once again, dialogue understood in this way becomes much more than simply the production of speech: it is revealed as intrinsically linked to the ability to mind-read.

Other uses of mind-reading

The importance of mind-reading for social understanding and communication has been emphasized because these are arguably the most important of its functions. However, there are several other functions of this crucial ability. Let us explore just a few here.

First, there is deception. Deception, of course, is all about making someone *believe* that something is true when it is actually false. Normal children begin to engage in very convincing deception soon after they understand the notion of false belief, around 4 years of age.[23]

Secondly, there is empathy. Mind-reading naturally confers on the child an ability to infer how someone might be interpreting events and how they may be feeling. For example, children of 3 years of age can understand another person's emotional state as caused by external situations and by around 5 years old they are adept at understanding a person's emotions in terms of what they *thought* was likely to happen (e.g.: "Jane is happy because she *thinks* she's won the race"), irrespective of whether their thought coincides with reality.[24]

A third spin-off of mind-reading is that it allows for self-consciousness or self-reflection. As soon as a child can attribute mental states to itself, it can begin to reflect on its own mind. Thus, 4 year olds succeed at distinguishing appearance from reality[25] and recognizing the fallibility of their beliefs ("I *thought* it was an [x], but maybe I was wrong"), and about the causes of their own behaviour ("I looked for my ball under the car because I *thought* that's where it was"), as well as the source of their knowledge ("I *know* it's Kate's birthday because mummy told me"). Clearly, this transforms their thoughts from a focus on the here-and-now to a focus on their own subjectivity. An added advantage of this is that they can rehearse possible solutions to problems in their own mind, before actually trying ("*Imagine* if I did [x]; would that work?" etc).

A fourth use of mind-reading is in teaching or attempting to change a person's mind, through persuasion, etc. The realization that other people's thoughts and beliefs are shaped by the information to which they are exposed allows for the possibility of *informing* others, in order to change what they *know* or how they *think*.

MINDBLINDNESS IN AUTISM

The ability to understand one's own and others' minds appears to occur quite spontaneously in childhood[26]. An increasing number of studies have shown, however, that children with autism have particular difficulties in reasoning about mental states and it has been proposed that this deficit underlies many of the developmental abnormalities that are characteristic of the disorder[27]. For example, on tests of false belief comprehension, children with autism make more errors than both normal and learning disabled children of a younger mental age.[28] Whilst most children with autism fail tests of belief understanding, a minority of them do pass. This subgroup ranges from 20–35% in different samples. But when these subjects are given a more taxing test of belief understanding (comprising understanding second-order, nested beliefs, or *beliefs about beliefs* (e.g.: of the form "Anne thinks that Sally thinks *x*") — these being well within the comprehension of normal 6–7 year old children — even many teenagers with autism fail outright.[29] It appears then, that whilst most children with autism do not understand beliefs even at the level of normal 3–4 year old children, some do; but these show impaired understanding of beliefs at the level of normal 6–7 year old children. Clearly, something is going wrong in their development of the concept of belief.

This inability of individuals with autism to understand others' beliefs reveals itself most dramatically on tests of deception.[30] As discussed earlier, since deception entails belief manipulation, this is consistent with their difficulties in belief comprehension. Thus, in the Penny Hiding Game,[31] a simple test of deception which requires the child to conceal a penny in one or other hand, children with autism fail to hide the clues that enable the guesser to infer the whereabouts of the penny.[32] For example, they omit to close the empty hand, or they hide the penny in full view of the guesser, or they show the guesser where the penny is, before he or she has guessed. In contrast, children with learning disabilities, and normal 3 year old children make far fewer errors of this sort.

What of their understanding of other mental states? When children with autism are asked how a story character will feel when given something they either *want* or *do not want*, few impairments are found, relative to other children of similar mental-age.[33] Understanding this simple aspect of desire thus seems to be within their ability. Similarly, on tests of understanding *perception*, children with autism have been tested at both levels of visual perspective-taking and appear to show few deficits.[34]

Another key set of mental states is emotion. In his early studies, Hobson[35] found that subjects with autism performed considerably worse than other groups on tasks involving the matching of emotional expressions. Other research has focused not on the recognition but on the prediction of emotions. The aim in these studies is to establish how much children with autism understand about the *causes* of emotion — how a person will feel, given a particular set of circumstances. As mentioned earlier, normal 3–4 year old children understand that emotion can be caused by *situations* (e.g.: nice situations make you feel happy, nasty ones make you feel sad) and *desires* (e.g.: fulfilled desires make you happy, unfulfilled ones make you feel sad). By 4–6 years old, normal children also understand that *beliefs* can affect emotion (e.g.: if you *think* you're getting what you want, you'll feel happy, and if you think you're not, you'll feel sad — irrespective of what you're actually getting).

Children with autism have been shown to be able to judge a story character's emotion when this was caused by a situation, and were as good as a group with learning difficulties at predicting the character's emotion given her desire. However, they were significantly worse at predicting the character's emotion given her belief, compared with normal 5 year old children or children with learning difficulties.[36] The implication is that "simple" emotions may be within the understanding of people with autism, whilst 'complex' emotions pose considerable difficulties.

Deficits in understanding pretence are also characteristic. Normally, pretend play is present from at least 2 years of age[37] but children with autism, with a verbal mental age well above 2 years, show little or no spontaneous pretence[38] They also produce significantly less spontaneous pretend play than learning disabled control groups.[39]

EXAMPLES FROM CLINICAL EXPERIENCE [40]

Mindblindness has far wider implications for development than experimental studies alone might indicate. Such difficulties continue to affect social and communicative functions well into adult life, as the following examples indicate:

(i) *Insensitivity to other people's* feelings

Frederick, a 12 year old boy with autism, had parents who were desperately anxious that he should be assimilated into his local secondary school. They were horrified to hear that in the first week he had approached the head-teacher in Assembly and commented on how many spots he had.

(ii) *Inability to take into account what other people* know

Jeffrey, an extremely able young man with autism who held a responsible position in a computing company, was unable to appreciate that if he had witnessed an event, this knowledge might not be shared by others. He was unable to comprehend that his experience was different from theirs, often referring to events without providing the essential background information necessary for colleagues to understand the context of his argument.

(iii) *Inability to negotiate friendships by reading and responding to* intentions

Samantha, a 10 year old girl with autism attending a mainstream school, had been carefully taught by her parents to say her name and address correctly. Apparently believing that this was all that was required in order to "make friends", she would march up to groups of children, solemnly recite her name and address and then hit out at the nearest child if this did not result in an immediate request to join in.

(iv) Inability to read the listener's level of interest in one's speech

Robert, a 12 year old boy, also attending mainstream school, constantly irritated peers and teachers alike by his "boring" monologues on the cubic capacity of Renault cars, structural details of the Severn Bridge, or albinism. He would discuss just these three topics at length with anyone and was quite unable to recognise that his enthusiasm for these arcane subjects was in no way shared.

(v) Inability to detect a speaker's intended meaning

In art class, David, a 14 year old with autism, was told by his teacher to paint the child next to him. Taking her at her word he did just that, much to the other child's distress.

Leo, a young man with a clerical job, also ran into difficulties because he would act literally on what was said. Thus, someone might well say to him in an exasperated tone "You do that again . . .!", and he would obligingly trot off and do so, this being in total opposition to the actual wishes of the speaker.

(vi) Inability to anticipate what other's might think of one's actions

Joseph, when a teenager, frequently regaled strangers with very personal details about himself, not realising that to talk to them about one's bodily functions, or the intimate details of family life, was inappropriate. He would also cause problems by taking off his clothes in public whenever the weather got hot, with no sense of embarrassment.

Although many of these problems improved as he grew older, difficulties arose again shortly after he started a job with a computer firm. He showed no sense of personal space and would hover over the desks of female employees or lean up against them in lifts or queues etc. After some weeks of this the secretarial staff demanded his dismissal on the grounds of sexual harassment.

(vii) *Inability to understand* misunderstandings

Michael, a young man with autism, was dismissed from his job after an incident in which he had attacked the cloakroom attendant. He showed absolutely no remorse for this, having hit her with his umbrella "because she gave me the wrong ticket". Being in the habit of doing everything meticulously himself he simply could not understand that others might make mistakes. Long afterwards he still expressed bewilderment that he had lost his job whereas, by rights, he was convinced the cloakroom attendant should have lost hers.

(viii) *Inability to deceive or understand* deception

John, a 25 year old man with autism, had a job working in a jewellers. Because he was recognised as being totally honest, he had access to the keys of the safe. However, his failure to understand deception left him open to exploitation by others and a new night watchman took advantage of the situation. Being asked casually for the keys one night John readily handed these over and when the night watchman, the keys and the contents of the safe had disappeared, he was charged with being an accessory to the robbery. Although these charges were dropped he could clearly no longer be employed in such a position of trust again.

(ix) *Inability to understand the* reasons *behind people's actions*

David, a 20 year old man with autism and of normal intelligence but with considerable social difficulties, was offered employment by his uncle. Taking into account David's particular pattern of social behaviour the uncle had, sensibly, found a niche for David in a quiet corner of the accounts office. Rather than being grateful for his uncle's efforts, David was outraged to learn that he had not instantly been made a managing director of the company. He walked out of the job after only a few days and thereafter harboured intense resentment against the one person who had tried so hard to help him.

(x) *Inability to understand* "unwritten rules" *or conventions*

Jan, a 25 year old man, had spent many months in a social skills group trying to improve his conversational and other social abilities. He had particular difficulties in making spontaneous comments, and the group leader had put in a lot of effort in trying to help him develop conversational "gambits", seek out topics of mutual interest or compliment people on their appearance. The day after he had attended his first dance he came in full of pride for the way he had been able to engage a young woman in conversation for much of the evening. "What sort of things did you say to her?" asked the group tutor, intrigued. Well I told her how nice she looked and how I really liked the colour of her red dress because it exactly matched her gums"!

These examples of different mind-reading *errors* by no means exhaust the many different problems that can occur in this area, but are sufficient to convey how people with autism often just fail to understand another person's actions or speech. They give some indication of the many social difficulties experienced by individuals with autism and how they may lead to rejection, isolation, misunderstandings and even abuse.

CAN MIND-READING BE TAUGHT?

Normal children do not seem to require explicit teaching in order to be able to mind-read. Nevertheless, it may be that it can be explicitly taught to children who have failed to acquire it naturally. Such teaching might provide an alternative route into mind-reading and hence prove a more effective way of helping children with autism to improve their social and communication skills.

Consider the analogy with congenitally blind children learning to read: Braille gives an alternative way into the problem of learning to decipher written words. We are interested in whether there might be an alternative way into the problem of learning to "read" minds. Blind children have no central cognitive deficit in their "word recognition system", but do have a sensory impairment which Braille circumvents. In contrast, children with autism are postulated to have no sensory impairment, but do have a central cognitive deficit, in their capacity for mind-reading. The task then, in trying to teach them to mind-read, may be considerably harder than teaching a blind child to read, since changing **understanding** is involved. Nevertheless, it is apparent that children with autism can be successfully taught to interpret mental states.

Recent studies indicate that they can learn to understand false beliefs,[41] or to distinguish between appearance and reality.[42] Teaching in these studies was conducted through a variety of media, including computers and real actors.[43] In addition, one study[44] used behavioural and emotional clues to help children understand false belief, while another[45] utilized a direct instruction approach to teach the appearance-reality distinction. These studies used repetition of the task, plus feedback, and the results were remarkably consistent. Almost all children with autism were able to learn to pass the tasks and, in some cases, maintain what they had learnt over a period of two months or more. However, generalization to untrained tasks, even if these were similar to the original ones, remained limited.

Existing studies, therefore, although offering some encouragement for therapeutic intervention, also raise a number of important questions.

- If mental-state concepts can be taught, which techniques facilitate learning?
- How much teaching is necessary and how long will the effects of teaching persist?
- Are some mental-state concepts (e.g. emotion or pretence), more difficult for children with autism to acquire than others (e.g. knowledge and belief)?
- Are mental states acquired in a strict sequence? That is, does acquisition of one concept (such as emotion) always precede the acquisition of another (such as belief). In other words, is understanding emotion a necessary precursor for understanding beliefs?
- If mental-state concepts are acquired through teaching on specific tasks does generalization occur to allow the child to understand novel examples of behaviour?
- Are mental-state concepts that are acquired through explicit teaching used in the same way as those acquired more naturally?
- Does acquisition of mental-state concepts lead to changes in other aspects of social and communicative behaviour? If so, which ones?
- What factors might account for some children acquiring mental-state terms and some failing to do so?

APPROACHES TO TEACHING MENTAL-STATE CONCEPTS

The following section briefly outlines the main principles underlying our teaching programme and summarises the overall results from our studies.[46] Subsequent chapters describe in detail the techniques and materials employed in teaching.

The teaching principles

- Teaching needs to be broken down into small steps, so that complex skills are acquired gradually, as a sequence of separate components.
- Normal developmental sequences are generally an important guide to the sequence of skill acquisition. Thus, skills that are acquired early by "normally" developing children are likely to be learned more rapidly than those acquired at later stages of development.
- Naturalistic teaching is usually more effective than teaching procedures that take little account of the child's normal environment or pay little heed to individual skills or interests.
- Behaviours that are systematically reinforced will be acquired more rapidly and will be more likely to be maintained than those that are not reinforced in this way. Although extrinsic reinforces (such as praise), are important for this

purpose, intrinsic rewards, that derive from the task itself, or the pleasure that comes from completing it successfully, are at least equally potent.

- By ensuring errorless learning (i.e. avoiding the opportunity for making mistakes as far as possible) the speed of task acquisition can be greatly increased.
- Problems of generalization (i.e. the failure to adapt learning to new situations or tasks), that frequently limit the success of teaching programmes, can be reduced if teaching focuses on the principles that underlie concepts, rather than relying on instruction alone.

The teaching approaches adopted in the study reported below were specifically designed to deal with these issues. It seemed possible that the limitations of earlier studies may have been due to the fact that, by concentrating teaching on the understanding of false beliefs, training was aimed at too complex a level. Thus, in order to minimise the conceptual complexity of the tasks, the understanding of mental states was divided into three separate components:

> understanding informational states
> understanding emotion
> understanding pretence

Each child was exposed to teaching on only one of these concepts. Then, each of the concepts was ordered into five successive levels of understanding. Level 1 being the simplest level and Level 5 the most difficult. Examples of these stages are presented in Table 1.1.

The stages of teaching were based on what is known about the development of mental state understanding in normal children[47] which ensured that the tasks followed a developmental sequence. In order to make learning as natural as possible the teaching environment was enhanced by using a broad range of methods, including play, pictures, computers and games. The tasks themselves were designed to be as rewarding as possible for the children and the materials used offered rapid and clear feedback on the child's performance. **Praise and encouragement were given at every stage**. If errors were made the child was immediately prompted with the correct response in order to avoid any perseveration of mistakes, or misunderstandings.

OVERCOMING PROBLEMS OF GENERALIZATION

Finally, teaching procedures attempted to overcome the "failure to generalize" phenomenon often evident in earlier studies. Evidence suggests that teaching children about the principles that underlie concepts is more effective than simple

Table 1.1 The five levels of mental state teaching

	EMOTION	BELIEF	PRETENCE
LEVEL 1	Photographic facial recognition (happy/sad/ angry/afraid)	Simple perspective-taking	Sensorimotor play
LEVEL 2	Schematic facial recognition (happy/sad/ angry/afraid)	Complex perspective-taking	Functional play (≤ 2 examples)
LEVEL 3	Situation-based emotions (happy/sad/ angry/afraid)	Seeing leads to knowing (self/other)	Functional play (>2 examples)
LEVEL 4	Desire-based emotions (happy/sad)	True belief/ action prediction	Pretend play (≤ 2 examples)
LEVEL 5	Belief-based emotions (happy/sad)	False belief	Pretend play (>2 examples)

Table 1.2 Some principles underlying fundamental mental state concepts

Perception causes knowledge: *A person will know x if s/he saw or heard about x* (e.g. Snow White doesn't know the apple is poisoned because she didn't see the witch put poison in it.)

Desires are satisfied by actions or objects: *If a person wants x, s/he will be happy to obtain x. Conversely, if a person doesn't get x, s/he will be unhappy.* The children want to go to the park and are happy when their mother takes them. They are not happy if they are taken to the supermarket instead.

Pretence involves object substitution or outcome suspension: *When a person pretends x, s/he does without the usual objects/consequences, just for fun.* (e.g. Alan holds a banana to his ear. He is pretending to talk on the telephone.)

instruction, as it helps them to generalize what they learn more effectively.[48] For many children, of course, such principles do not need to be made explicit but when there is a failure to learn by normal means, as is the case for children with autism, these principles may need to be taught "inductively", through intensive training with many examples and by means of a variety of different techniques (eg: dolls and puppet stories, role-play, picture stories, etc.). In the present study children were provided with *general* principles in order to help them learn specific mental state concepts.[49] In doing so an attempt was made to formalize, and make explicit, principles that in normal development are presumably implicit.[50,51] Examples of such principles for some fundamental mental stages (know, desire and think) are presented in Table 1.2.

OUTCOME OF THE EXPERIMENTAL STUDY

We were surprised to find that significant changes occurred in the specific areas selected after only a relatively brief training period, and that these improvements were maintained long after intervention ceased. We suspect that a longer training period, together with the involvement of families, as well as teachers could enhance the effectiveness of the methods used even further. For this reason, and as a response to requests from parents and teachers, we have compiled this Guide, to share our approaches to teaching.

FOR WHOM IS THE MANUAL DESIGNED?

The experimental study on which this manual is based involved young children with autism, aged between 4 and 13 years, with a language age of at least a 5 year old level. This is the linguistic level at which normal children clearly demonstrate the ability to read minds. The materials were all constructed with this age and ability group in mind, but there is no reason why the materials should not be adapted for use with older groups of subjects, as long as they have reached these minimum levels of ability. Hence, although "children" are referred to throughout the text, with appropriate modifications (especially to play materials etc) the procedures could be adapted relatively easily to meet the needs of older clients.

THE LIMITATIONS OF TEACHING APPROACHES OF THIS KIND

Successful educational and intervention programmes for children with autism require many different strategies and approaches. Furthermore, teaching procedures will always need to be modified according to the individual child's skills, interests, and difficulties. There are no simple "recipe books" that can be used to overcome the fundamental disabilities in autism, and this Guide makes no claim to offer a comprehensive approach for teaching children about beliefs, emotions or imagination.

Understanding — and reacting appropriately to — people's emotions, involves more than the ability to recognise a few clear and relatively simple emotions from pictures or cartoons. Whether a situation is construed as being happy, sad or frightening will depend, not only on the current context but on the past history of the individual(s) involved. Moreover, facial expression alone may not always be a true representation of how someone is feeling — a smile, for example may be used in a brave attempt to disguise sadness or pain. And, being able to recognise certain unambiguous emotions in other people, may not necessarily help children with autism fully understand or cope with their own emotional responses, especially if these differ from those of others. Christmas celebrations, birthday parties, time off school, may all produce great anxiety in a child with autism, and this will obviously conflict with the expressions of pleasure shown by other children at such times.

Similarly, play entails not just the ability to use toys appropriately, but, as soon as interactions with other children are involved, will also require many different levels of social and cognitive skills.

Such complexities cannot be addressed using pre-packaged teaching materials, and far more sophisticated and individualised teaching strategies will be needed once the child approaches these higher levels of competence. However, in the early stages of skill acquisition, simple materials and teaching techniques can play an invaluable role. It is for children, or older individuals, who are at the threshold of development in the domains of understanding beliefs, emotions or pretence that this Guide is designed.

THE STRUCTURE OF THE GUIDE

The following four chapters of the Guide are organised into three main parts; one for each of the 3 classes of mental state concepts taught in our experimental study. **Emotion, Informational States, and Play.**

Each section provides details on:

- how to assess the level of skill shown by the individual child
- how to establish a baseline (i.e. to determine the level at which teaching should commence)
- the materials to be used at each stage
- the teaching procedures to be followed.

Advice on teaching procedures includes the **general principles** that need to be established as well as specific teaching examples. The materials and guidance for teaching the understanding of Emotion and Informational States are much more specific than those for teaching Pretend Play. In this latter area the child's own individual interests need to be followed as far as possible in order for real progress to be made. However, in all sections, suggestions about materials and teaching strategies are only meant to provide **guidelines** for teachers; they are not meant to be either prescriptive or restrictive. Instead, teachers should naturally use their creativity whenever possible and base teaching procedures around strategies with which they are comfortable, selecting materials that, in their experience, are likely to be of particular interest for the individual children with whom they are working.

To measure progress, there are **Record Forms** for each of the three areas taught. These also provide a framework for the teaching programme as a whole and should be completed at the end of every session (See Appendix 1.1). Scoring allows for responses that are correct or incorrect as well as those that are idiosyncratic, partially correct or difficult to code.

At every stage of the programme it is crucial to reinforce the child's attempts to co-operate. This can be done in many different ways; for example by ensuring that the materials used are as interesting as possible, making sure that the teacher appears enthusiastic about what they are doing; always reinforcing correct answers during training or quickly prompting the correct ones if the child makes a mistake. Except during the initial assessment stages the child should be given consistent feedback and help and never be allowed to "flounder" without guidance or support. At the end of the session an additional reward (allowing the child to do something he or she enjoys, which may or may not have anything to do with the teaching procedures) should be provided. It is important, of course to remember that, by definition, a reinforcer is an event that strengthens the probability of a behaviour occurring again and that what is reinforcing for a child with autism may be very different from the rewards that work well with other children. Thus, silence, rather than praise; being left alone for a while or being allowed to spend some time in obsessional or ritualistic activities may all be much more effective than more "conventional" rewards.

Teaching sessions should always begin with an activity that is already well established, before training on more difficult tasks begins.

REFERENCES AND NOTES

1. Lord, C. and Rutter, M. (1994). Autism and pervasive developmental disorders. In M. Rutter, E. Taylor, and L. Hersov (Eds) *Child and Adolescent Psychiatry* (3rd Ed.). Oxford: Blackwell.

2. Frith, U. (1989). *Autism: Explaining the Enigma.* Oxford: Basil Blackwell.

3. Howlin, P. and Rutter, M. (1987). *Treatment of Autistic Children.* Chichester: Wiley.

4. Howlin, P. (1989). Changing approaches to communication training with autistic children. *British Journal of Disorders of Communication,* **24**, 151–168.

5. Howlin, P. and Rutter, M. (1987). Ibid. and Schopler, E., Mesibov, G. (1986). *Social Behavior in Autism.* New York: Plenum.

6. Schuler, A. (1989). The socialization of autistic children. Paper presented at International Conference on Educational Issues in Autism. August; Mons, Belgium.

7. Taras, M., Matson, J. and Leary, C. (1988). Training social interpersonal skills in two autistic children. *Journal of Behaviour Therapy and Experimental Psychiatry.* **19**, 275–280.

8. Howlin, P. and Rutter, M. (1987). Ibid.

9. Howlin, P. (1987). An overview of social behaviour in autism. In E. Schopler and G. Mesibov (Eds) *Social Behavior in Autism.* New York: Plenum.

10. This section is adapted from Baron-Cohen, S. (1994). The development of a theory of mind: Where would we be without the Internal Stance? In M. Rutter and D. Hay (Eds) *Developmental Principles and Clinical Issues in Psychology and Child Psychiatry.* Oxford: Blackwell.

11. Wellman, H.M. (1990). *The Child's Theory of Mind.* Cambridge: MIT Press.

12. Bretherton, I. and Beeghly, M. (1982). Talking about internal states: The acquisition of an explicit theory of mind. *Developmental Psychology,* **18**, 906–921.

13. Dennett, D. (1978). Beliefs about beliefs. *Behavioral and Brain Sciences,* **4**, 759–770.

14. Wimmer, H. and Perner, J. (1983). Beliefs about beliefs: Representation and constraining function of wrong beliefs in young children's understanding of deception. *Cognition,* **13**, 103–128.

15. Baron-Cohen, S., Leslie, A.M. and Frith, U. (1985). Does the autistic child have a "theory of mind?" *Cognition,* **21**, 27–43.

16. Flavell, J.H., Shipstead, S. and Croft, K. (1978). Young children's knowledge about visual perception: hiding objects from others. *Child Development,* **49**, 1208–1211.

17. Pratt, C. and Bryant, P. (1990). Young children understand that looking leads to knowing (so long as they are looking into a single barrel). *Child Development,* **61**, 973–982.

18. Wellman, H.M. (1990) Ibid.

19. Bates, E., Benigni, L., Bretherton, I., Camaioni, L. and Volterra, V. (1979). Cognition and communication from 9–13 months: correlational findings. In E.D. Bates (Ed). *The Emergence of Symbols: Cognition and Communication in Infancy*. New York: Academic Press.

20. Wellman, H.M. (1990) Ibid.

21. Dennett, D. (1978). *Brainstorms: Philosophical Essays on Mind and Psychology*. Brighton: Harvester Press.

22. Grice, H. P. (1975). Logic and Conversation: In R. Cole and J. Morgan (Eds) *Syntax and Semantics: Speech Acts*. New York: Academic Press.

23. Sodian, B., Taylor, C., Harris, P.L. and Perner, J. (1991). Early deception and the child's theory of mind: false trails and genuine markers. *Child Development*, **62**, 468–483.

24. Harris, P.L. (1989). *Children and Emotion*. Oxford: Basil Blackwell.

25. Flavell, J.H., Flavell, E.R. and Green, F.L. (1987) Young children's knowledge about the apparent–real and pretend–real distinctions. *Development Psychology*, **23**, 816–822.

26. Perner, J. (1991). *Understanding the Representational Mind*. Cambridge, Mass: MIT Press.

27. Baron-Cohen, S., Tager-Flusberg, H. and Cohen, D.J. (Eds) (1993). *Understanding Other Minds*. Oxford: Oxford University Press. See also Baron-Cohen, S. (1995) *Mindblindness*. Cambridge, Mass.: MIT Press.

28. Baron-Cohen, S., Leslie, A. M. and Frith, U. (1985). Ibid.

29. Baron-Cohen, S. (1989). The autistic child's theory of mind: a case of specific language delay. *Journal of Child Psychology and Psychiatry*, **30**, 285–298.

30. Sodian, B. and Frith, U. (1992). Deception and sabotage in autistic, retarded and normal children. *Journal of Child Psychology and Psychiatry*, **33**, 591–605.

31. Gratch, G. (1964). Response alteration in children: a developmental study of orientations to uncertainty. *Vita Humana*, **7**, 49–60.

32. Baron-Cohen, S. (1992). Out of sight or out of mind? Another look at deception in autism. *Journal of Child Psychology and Psychiatry*, **33**, 1141–1155.

33. Baron-Cohen, S. (1991). Do people with autism understand what causes emotion? *Child Development*, **62**, 385–395.

34. Tan, J. and Harris, P. (1991). Autistic children understand seeing and wanting. *Development and Psychopathology*, **3**, 163–174.

35. Hobson, P.R. (1986a). The autistic child's appraisal of expressions of emotion. *Journal of Child Psychology and Psychiatry*, **27**, 321–342.
    —(1986b). The autistic child's appraisal of expressions of emotion: A further study. *Journal of Child Psychology and Psychiatry*, **27**, 671–680.

36. Baron-Cohen, S. (1991). Ibid.

37. Fein, G.G. (1981). Pretend play in childhood: an integrative review. *Child Development*, **52**, 1095–1118.

38. Baron-Cohen, S. (1987). Autism and symbolic play. *British Journal of Developmental Psychology*, **5**, 139–148.

39. Ungerer, J.A. and Sigman, M. (1981). Symbolic play and language compre-

hension in autistic children. *Journal of the American Academy of Child and Adolescent Psychiatry*, **20**, 318–337.

40. This section is adapted from Baron-Cohen, S. and Howlin, P. (1993). The theory of mind deficit in autism: Some questions for teaching and diagnosis. In S. Baron-Cohen et al. (Eds) Ibid.

41. Bowler, D.M., Stromm, E. and Urquhart, L. (1993). Elicitation of first-order "theory of mind" in children with autism. Unpublished manuscript, Department of Psychology, City University, London.

42. Starr, E. (1993). Teaching the appearance–reality distinction to children with autism. Paper presented at the British Psychological Society Developmental Psychology Section Annual Conference, Birmingham.

43. Swettenham, J.S. (1991). The autistic child's theory of mind: a computer-based investigation. Unpublished D.Phil thesis, University of York.

44. Bower, D.M., Stromm, E., and Urquhart, L. (1993). Ibid.

45. Starr, E. (1993). Ibid.

46. Hadwin, J., Baron-Cohen, S., Howlin, P. and Hill, K. (1996). Can children with autism be taught concepts of emotion, belief and pretence? *Development and Psychopathology*.

47. Wellman, H.M. (1990). Ibid.

48. Perry, M. (1991). Learning and transfer: Instructional conditions and conceptual change. *Cognitive Development*, **6**, 449–468.

49. Baron-Cohen, S. and Howlin, P. (1993). The theory of mind deficit in autism: Some questions for teaching and diagnosis. In S. Baron-Cohen et al. (Eds) Ibid.

50. Perner, J. (1991). Ibid.

51. Wellman, H.M. (1990). Ibid.

Part II
Teaching about Emotions

In this section we describe five levels of emotional understanding that can be taught.

THE FIVE LEVELS OF EMOTIONAL UNDERSTANDING

Level 1. Recognition of facial expression from photographs
This is the ability to recognise, from *photographs*, facial expressions such as happy, sad, angry, and afraid.

Level 2. Recognition of emotion from schematic drawings
This is scored if the child is able to identify the correct face from four facial *cartoons*: happy, sad, angry, and afraid, in the same way as above.

Level 3. Identification of situation-based emotions
These are emotions triggered by situations (e.g. fear when an accident is about to occur). At this level the child should be able to predict how a character will feel, given the obvious emotional content of the picture.

Level 4. Desire-based emotions
These are emotions caused by a person's desire being fulfilled or unfulfilled. At this level the child should be able to identify a character's feelings (either happy or sad) according to whether his or her wishes are fulfilled or not.

Level 5. Belief-based emotions
These are emotions caused by what someone *thinks* is the case, even if what they think conflicts with reality. The child is required to follow a sequence of three pictures and to interpret the feeling that cartoon characters will experience according to whether they believe their desires have been satisfied or not.

   The following sections describe how to assess and teach at each of these levels.

LEVEL 1. RECOGNIZING FACIAL EXPRESSION FROM PHOTOGRAPHS

Level 1 is scored if the child can recognise, from *photographs*, facial expressions of the four emotions: happy, sad, angry, and afraid.

Materials and assessment procedures

Four black-and-white photographs of people with happy, sad, angry or fearful expressions. Matching photographs (on laminated cards) for the child. The materials can also be adapted so that the child's faces can be made into "stickers" or attached with Velcro in order to make the matching task more interesting.

Figure 2.1 Photographic facial expressions of emotion (reproduced with kind permission from Ekman and Friesen, 1975, *Unmasking the Face*, copyright © Paul Ekman 1975).

Teacher: Choose one of the four facial expressions and ask the child to point to it.

Emotion Question: Can you point to the happy/sad/angry/afraid face?
Prompt — show me where the happy/sad/angry/afraid person is.

Establishing a baseline

Present the four photographs to the child.

<u>Say</u>   **Now we are going to look at some faces that show us how people feel.**
<u>Ask</u>   **Can you point to the [happy] face?**

If a child fails to recognise any of the four emotions shown in the photographs start teaching at this level.

Teaching procedures

Children are asked to identify the four photographic facial expressions of emotion (happy/sad/angry/afraid) in turn (randomized).

The teacher first places the set of photos on the table and names the emotion shown in each one of these. The child is then asked to match his or her faces to those displayed by the teacher.

Let's put the four faces here. There is happy, sad, angry and afraid.
I have some more faces for you to look at. Can you put these with the pictures that look the same?

This one is happy. Where should we put the happy face?

Yes, that's right, that face is happy too! etc . . .

The task is made easy for the child by the teacher providing a model initially. If errors are made at any point the child is immediately provided with the correct answer.

LEVEL 2. RECOGNIZING EMOTION FROM SCHEMATIC DRAWINGS

This is scored if the child is able to identify the correct face from four facial *cartoons*: happy, sad, angry, and afraid, in the same way as above.

Materials and assessment procedures

Four black-and-white line drawings of people with happy, sad, angry or fearful expressions. Matching faces for the child which might be drawn on stickers or attached with Velcro, etc.

Figure 2.2 Schematic facial expressions of emotion (adapted from Hobson, 1989)

Establishing a baseline

Present the four cartoons to the child.

> <u>Say</u>   **Now we are going to look at some faces that show us how
> people feel.**
> <u>Ask</u>   **Can you point to the [happy] face?**

If a child fails to recognise any one of the four emotions shown in the drawings
start teaching at this level.

Teaching procedures

Children are asked to identify the four black-and-white cartoon facial expressions
of emotion (happy/sad/angry/afraid) in turn (randomized).

The teacher first places the set of pictures on the table and names the emotion
shown in each one of these. The child is then asked to match his or her faces to
those placed by the teacher.

> **Let's put the four faces here. This is happy, sad, angry and afraid.**
> **I have some more faces for you to look at. Can you put these with**
> **the pictures that look the same?**
> **This one is happy. Where should we put the happy face?**
> **Yes, that's right, that face is happy too! etc . . .**

The task is made easy for the child by the teacher providing a model initially. If
errors are made at any point the child is immediately provided with the correct
answer.

LEVEL 3. IDENTIFYING "SITUATION-BASED" EMOTIONS

Situation-based emotions are emotions that are triggered by situations (e.g. fear when an accident is about to occur). At this level the child should be able to predict how a character will feel, given the emotional content of the picture.

Materials and assessment procedures

A set of four cartoon faces as in the previous section, together with a set of pictures, indicating a variety of emotional situations. The child needs to interpret the social and emotional context of the picture and predict what the emotional expression of the characters will be. The situations indicate **FEAR, HAPPINESS, SADNESS OR ANGER.** Sometimes there is an equally plausible correct alternative answer (for example, some of the "sad" stories might also invoke an "angry" response) and if so the teacher should use his or her own judgement in scoring.

Establishing a baseline

To assess situation-based emotion, pick one story from each of the emotion sections listed below (i.e. four in all). The following example illustrates how to administer the stories.

Situation: The big dog is chasing Dan down the road (Example 1).
Present the picture to the child.

<u>Say</u>: **Look, the big dog is chasing Dan down the road.**

<u>Emotion Question</u>: **How will Dan feel when the big dog chases him? Will he feel happy, sad, angry or frightened?**

Point to each of the faces in turn.

Let's see how Dan feels. The child can point to a face.
Look, Dan is frightened.

<u>Why Question</u>: **Why is he frightened?**

If a child fails to answer either the *Emotion* or the *Why* question without prompts, on any one of the four situational emotion stories you have chosen, then start teaching at this level.

Teaching procedures

From the set of pictures provided (see following pages) the teacher selects ones that reflect the four different emotions (happy, sad, angry, afraid). There are twelve different pictures for each emotion.

The teacher shows the picture to the child and describes what is happening.

Then s/he asks a question about how the character in the picture will feel, prompting with the four possible alternatives (i.e. "Will s/he feel happy, sad, angry or afraid?"). The child is encouraged to point to the correct picture.

If the response is correct the teacher reinforces this and strengthens the child's understanding by asking "Why is he happy/sad etc?" If the response is incorrect, the correct answer is provided, as is the reason for the character feeling this way.

Example of a situational emotion story (Example 22): Thomas sees the clowns at the circus.

Present the picture to the child.
Look, Thomas sees the clowns at the circus.

Emotion Question: **How will Thomas feel when he sees the clowns?**

PROMPT: Will he feel happy, sad, angry, or frightened? (vary the order in which the emotions are named). *Point to each of the faces in turn.*

Let's see how Thomas feels. The child can point to the faces.
Look, Thomas is happy.

Why Question: **Why is he happy?**

Teaching

Emotion Question: For an incorrect response.

Let's have a look and see how Thomas feels.

Look, Thomas is happy. *Point to Thomas's face.*
He is happy because he sees the clowns. *Point to the clowns.*
Thomas is happy because he sees the clowns at the circus. *Point to Thomas.*

General teaching principle

Whether correct or incorrect, the child is always provided with the general principle underlying that emotion.

> **When someone gives you something nice/you do something exciting (etc.), then you feel happy.**
>
> **When something scary happens, you feel frightened and want to run away/hide.**
>
> **When something nasty happens accidentally/people leave (etc.), then you feel sad.**
>
> **When someone does something nasty to you on purpose (etc.), then you feel angry.**

Figure 2.3 Nos 1–48
Picture and procedures used in identifying "situation-based" emotions

Frightening Situations
Teacher: Describe the picture to the child and ask the child either to <u>say</u> how the person in the story feels, or to <u>point</u> to one of the emotion faces below.

Picture 1: The big dog is chasing Dan down the road.

<u>Emotion Question</u>: How will Dan feel when the dog chases him?
prompt — will he feel happy/sad/angry/afraid?

<u>Justification Question</u>: Why will he feel happy/sad/angry/afraid?

Teacher: Describe the picture to the child and ask the child either to <u>say</u> how the person in the story feels, or to <u>point</u> to one of the emotion faces below.

Picture 2: The snake is sliding towards Harry's legs.

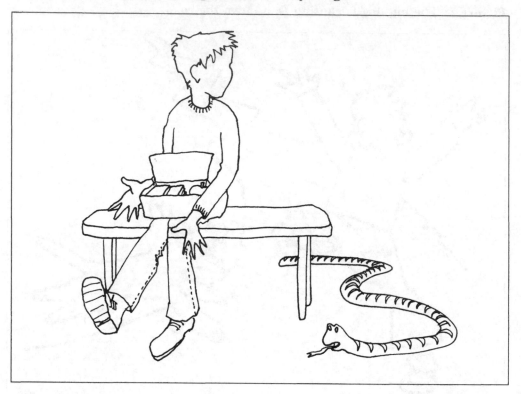

<u>Emotion Question</u>: How will Harry feel when the snake slides towards him?
prompt — will he feel happy/sad/angry/afraid?

<u>Justification Question</u>: Why will he feel happy/sad/angry/afraid?

Teacher: Describe the picture to the child and ask the child either to <u>say</u> how the person in the story feels, or to <u>point</u> to one of the emotion faces below.

Picture 3: Laura runs from the mouse in the kitchen.

<u>Emotion Question</u>: How will Laura feel when she runs from the mouse?
prompt — will she feel happy/sad/angry/afraid?

<u>Justification Question</u>: Why will she feel happy/sad/angry/afraid?

Teacher: Describe the picture to the child and ask the child either to <u>say</u> how the person in the story feels, or to <u>point</u> to one of the emotion faces below.

Picture 4: The spider is crawling towards Susan's chair.

<u>Emotion Question</u>: How will Susan feel when the spider crawls towards her chair? *prompt — will she feel happy/sad/angry/afraid?*

<u>Justification Question</u>: Why will she feel happy/sad/angry/afraid?

Teacher: Describe the picture to the child and ask the child either to <u>say</u> how the person in the story feels, or to <u>point</u> to one of the emotion faces below.

Picture 5: The shadow on the wall looks like a monster.

<u>Emotion Question</u>: How will Tony feel when the shadow looks like a monster?
prompt — will he feel happy/sad/angry/afraid?

<u>Justification Question</u>: Why will he feel happy/sad/angry/afraid?

Teacher: Describe the picture to the child and ask the child either to <u>say</u> how the person in the story feels, or to <u>point</u> to one of the emotion faces below.

Picture 6: Becky is lost in the woods. It is getting dark.

<u>Emotion Question</u>: How will Becky feel when she is lost in the woods?
prompt — will she feel happy/sad/angry/afraid?

<u>Justification Question</u>: Why will she feel happy/sad/angry/afraid?

Teacher: Describe the picture to the child and ask the child either to <u>say</u> how the person in the story feels, or to <u>point</u> to one of the emotion faces below.

Picture 7: Carl has lost his mummy in the shop.

<u>Emotion Question</u>: How will Carl feel when he has lost his mummy in the shop?
prompt — will he feel happy/sad/angry/afraid?

<u>Justification Question</u>: Why will he feel happy/sad/angry/afraid?

Teacher: Describe the picture to the child and ask the child either to <u>say</u> how the person in the story feels, or to <u>point</u> to one of the emotion faces below.

Picture 8: Sharon arrives home. The house is dark and empty.

<u>Emotion Question</u>: How will Sharon feel when the house is dark and empty? *prompt — will she feel happy/sad/angry/afraid?*

<u>Justification Question</u>: Why will she feel happy/sad/angry/afraid?

Teacher: Describe the picture to the child and ask the child either to <u>say</u> how the person in the story feels, or to <u>point</u> to one of the emotion faces below.

Picture 9: Fiona is stuck in a tree. She may fall.

<u>Emotion Question</u>: How will Fiona feel when she is stuck in the tree?
prompt — will she feel happy/sad/angry/afraid?

<u>Justification Question</u>: Why will she feel happy/sad/angry/afraid?

Teacher: Describe the picture to the child and ask the child either to __say__ how the person in the story feels, or to __point__ to one of the emotion faces below.

Picture 10: The truck is driving fast towards Bobby.

<u>Emotion Question</u>: How will Bobby feel when the truck is driving towards him? *prompt — will he feel happy/sad/angry/afraid?*

<u>Justification Question</u>: Why will he feel happy/sad/angry/afraid?

Teacher: Describe the picture to the child and ask the child either to <u>say</u> how the person in the story feels, or to <u>point</u> to one of the emotion faces below.

Picture 11: Lesley is waiting for the fireman to rescue her.

<u>Emotion Question</u>: How will Lesley feel when she is waiting for the fireman? *prompt — will she feel happy/sad/angry/afraid?*

<u>Justification Question</u>: Why will she feel happy/sad/angry/afraid?

Teacher: Describe the picture to the child and ask the child either to <u>say</u> how the person in the story feels, or to <u>point</u> to one of the emotion faces below.

Picture 12: Jamie is in the car. The barrier comes down. The train is coming.

<u>Emotion Question</u>: How will Jamie feel when the train is coming?
prompt — will he feel happy/sad/angry/afraid?

<u>Justification Question</u>: Why will he feel happy/sad/angry/afraid?

Happy Situations

Teacher: Describe the picture to the child and ask the child either to <u>say</u> how the person in the story feels, or to <u>point</u> to one of the emotion faces below.

Picture 13: Jennifer's daddy gives her cake for tea.

<u>Emotion Question</u>: How will Jennifer feel when daddy gives her cake for tea? *prompt — will she feel happy/sad/angry/afraid?*

<u>Justification Question</u>: Why will she feel happy/sad/angry/afraid?

Teacher: Describe the picture to the child and ask the child either to <u>say</u> how the person in the story feels, or to <u>point</u> to one of the emotion faces below.

Picture 14: Sam's mum has bought him a tin of paints.

<u>Emotion Question</u>: How will Sam feel when mum gives him a tin of paints?
prompt — will he feel happy/sad/angry/afraid?

<u>Justification Question</u>: Why will he feel happy/sad/angry/afraid?

Teacher: Describe the picture to the child and ask the child either to <u>say</u> how the person in the story feels, or to <u>point</u> to one of the emotion faces below.

Picture 15: Betty's grandma gives her a teddy for her birthday.

<u>Emotion Question</u>: How will Betty feel when grandma gives her a teddy?
prompt — will she feel happy/sad/angry/afraid?

<u>Justification Question</u>: Why will she feel happy/sad/angry/afraid?

Teacher: Describe the picture to the child and ask the child either to <u>say</u> how the person in the story feels, or to <u>point</u> to one of the emotion faces below.

Picture 16: Alan's daddy buys him a chocolate ice-cream.

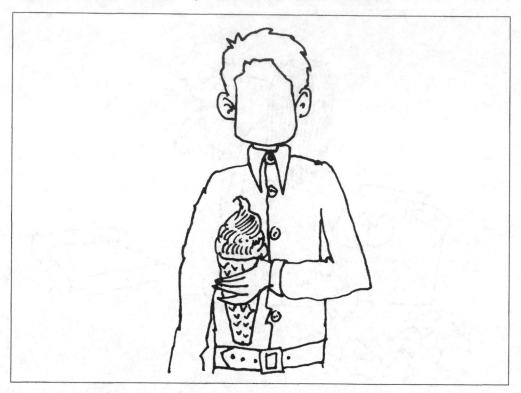

<u>Emotion Question</u>: How will Alan feel when daddy buys him an ice-cream?
prompt — will he feel happy/sad/angry/afraid?

<u>Justification Question</u>: Why will he feel happy/sad/angry/afraid?

Teacher: Describe the picture to the child and ask the child either to <u>say</u> how the person in the story feels, or to <u>point</u> to one of the emotion faces below.

Picture 17: Matthew's brother gives him a toy aeroplane.

<u>Emotion Question</u>: How will Matthew feel when his brother gives him an aeroplane?
prompt — will he feel happy/sad/angry/afraid?

<u>Justification Question</u>: Why will he feel happy/sad/angry/afraid?

Teacher: Describe the picture to the child and ask the child either to <u>say</u> how the person in the story feels, or to <u>point</u> to one of the emotion faces below.

Picture 18: Tina's sister buys her a picture of some flowers.

<u>Emotion Question</u>: How will Tina feel when her sister buys her a flower picture? *prompt — will she feel happy/sad/angry/afraid?*

<u>Justification Question</u>: Why will she feel happy/sad/angry/afraid?

Teacher: Describe the picture to the child and ask the child either to <u>say</u> how the person in the story feels, or to <u>point</u> to one of the emotion faces below.

Picture 19: Elizabeth pushes Jane up and down on the swing.

<u>Emotion Question</u>: How will Jane feel when Elizabeth pushes her up and down? *prompt — will she feel happy/sad/angry/afraid?*

<u>Justification Question</u>: Why will she feel happy/sad/angry/afraid?

Teacher: Describe the picture to the child and ask the child either to <u>say</u> how the person in the story feels, or to <u>point</u> to one of the emotion faces below.

Picture 20: Josie and Nigel go to the birthday party.

<u>Emotion Question</u>: How will Josie feel when she and Nigel go the party?
prompt — will she feel happy/sad/angry/afraid?

<u>Justification Question</u>: Why will she feel happy/sad/angry/afraid?

Teacher: Describe the picture to the child and ask the child either to <u>say</u> how the person in the story feels, or to <u>point</u> to one of the emotion faces below.

Picture 21: Daniel's mummy asks him to ride to the shops.

<u>Emotion Question</u>: How will Daniel feel when he rides to the shops*?*
prompt — will he feel happy/sad/angry/afraid?

<u>Justification Question</u>: Why will he feel happy/sad/angry/afraid?

Teacher: Describe the picture to the child and ask the child either to <u>say</u> how the person in the story feels, or to <u>point</u> to one of the emotion faces below.

Picture 22: Thomas sees the clowns at the circus.

<u>Emotion Question</u>: How will Thomas feel when he sees the clowns?
prompt — will he feel happy/sad/angry/afraid?

<u>Justification Question</u>: Why will he feel happy/sad/angry/afraid?

Teacher: Describe the picture to the child and ask the child either to <u>say</u> how the person in the story feels, or to <u>point</u> to one of the emotion faces below.

Picture 23: Katie has caught a big fish in the sea.

<u>Emotion Question</u>: How will Katie feel when she catches a big fish?
prompt — will she feel happy/sad/angry/afraid?

<u>Justification Question</u>: Why will she feel happy/sad/angry/afraid?

Teacher: Describe the picture to the child and ask the child either to <u>say</u> how the person in the story feels, or to <u>point</u> to one of the emotion faces below.

Picture 24: Billy is going round and round on the horse.

<u>Emotion Question</u>: How will Billy feel when he goes round and round on the horse? *prompt — will he feel happy/sad/angry/afraid?*

<u>Justification Question</u>: Why will he feel happy/sad/angry/afraid?

Sad Situations
Teacher: Describe the picture to the child and ask the child either to <u>say</u> how the person in the story feels, or to <u>point</u> to one of the emotion faces below.

Picture 25: Joanne cannot play on her swing. It's broken.

<u>Emotion Question</u>: How will Joanne feel when her swing is broken?
prompt — will she feel happy/sad/angry/afraid?

<u>Justification Question</u>: Why will she feel happy/sad/angry/afraid?

Teacher: Describe the picture to the child and ask the child either to <u>say</u> how the person in the story feels, or to <u>point</u> to one of the emotion faces below.

Picture 26: The seat and handles have fallen off Marie's bike.

<u>Emotion Question</u>: How will Marie feel when the seat and handles fall off her bike? *prompt — will she feel happy/sad/angry/afraid?*

<u>Justification Question</u>: Why will she feel happy/sad/angry/afraid?

Teacher: Describe the picture to the child and ask the child either to <u>say</u> how the person in the story feels, or to <u>point</u> to one of the emotion faces below.

Picture 27: Burt falls and smashes his plane on the floor.

<u>Emotion Question</u>: How will Burt feel when he smashes his plane?
prompt — will he feel happy/sad/angry/afraid?

<u>Justification Question</u>: Why will he feel happy/sad/angry/afraid?

Teacher: Describe the picture to the child and ask the child either to <u>say</u> how the person in the story feels, or to <u>point</u> to one of the emotion faces below.

Picture 28: Andrew drops his glass of juice. It shatters.

<u>Emotion Question</u>: How will Andrew feel when he drops his glass of juice?
prompt — will he feel happy/sad/angry/afraid?

<u>Justification Question</u>: Why will he feel happy/sad/angry/afraid?

Teacher: Describe the picture to the child and ask the child either to <u>say</u> how the person in the story feels, or to <u>point</u> to one of the emotion faces below.

Picture 29: Kim's daddy has to go away on a trip.

<u>Emotion Question</u>: How will Kim feel when her daddy goes away on a trip?
prompt — will she feel happy/sad/angry/afraid?

<u>Justification Question</u>: Why will she feel happy/sad/angry/afraid?

Teacher: Describe the picture to the child and ask the child either to <u>say</u> how the person in the story feels, or to <u>point</u> to one of the emotion faces below.

Picture 30: Lawrence is ill, he cannot go shopping with his mum.

<u>Emotion Question</u>: How will Lawrence feel when he cannot go shopping?
prompt — will he feel happy/sad/angry/afraid?

<u>Justification Question</u>: Why will he feel happy/sad/angry/afraid?

Teacher: Describe the picture to the child and ask the child either to <u>say</u> how the person in the story feels, or to <u>point</u> to one of the emotion faces below.

Picture 31: It's time for Adam's granddad to go home.

<u>Emotion Question</u>: How will Adam feel when his granddad goes home?
prompt — will he feel happy/sad/angry/afraid?

<u>Justification Question</u>: Why will he feel happy/sad/angry/afraid?

Teacher: Describe the picture to the child and ask the child either to <u>say</u> how the person in the story feels, or to <u>point</u> to one of the emotion faces below.

Picture 32: It's Amy's first day at school. Mummy is leaving.

<u>Emotion Question</u>: How will Amy feel when mummy leaves?
prompt — will she feel happy/sad/angry/afraid?

<u>Justification Question</u>: Why will she feel happy/sad/angry/afraid?

Teacher: Describe the picture to the child and ask the child either to <u>say</u> how the person in the story feels, or to <u>point</u> to one of the emotion faces below.

Picture 33: Sarah's kite has blown away in the wind.

<u>Emotion Question</u>: How will Sarah feel when her kite blows away?
prompt — will she feel happy/sad/angry/afraid?

<u>Justification Question</u>: Why will she feel happy/sad/angry/afraid?

Teacher: Describe the picture to the child and ask the child either to <u>say</u> how the person in the story feels, or to <u>point</u> to one of the emotion faces below.

Picture 34: The waves have washed Helen's sand-castle away.

<u>Emotion Question</u>: How will Helen feel when her sand-castle is washed away? *prompt — will she feel happy/sad/angry/afraid?*

<u>Justification Question</u>: Why will she feel happy/sad/angry/afraid?

Teacher: Describe the picture to the child and ask the child either to <u>say</u> how the person in the story feels, or to <u>point</u> to one of the emotion faces below.

Picture 35: The heavy rain has spoilt Frank's picture.

<u>Emotion Question</u>: How will Frank feel when his picture is spoilt?
prompt — will he feel happy/sad/angry/afraid?

<u>Justification Question</u>: Why will he feel happy/sad/angry/afraid?

Teacher: Describe the picture to the child and ask the child either to <u>say</u> how the person in the story feels, or to <u>point</u> to one of the emotion faces below.

Picture 36: Howard is walking the dog. It runs away.

<u>Emotion Question</u>: How will Howard feel when the dog runs away?
prompt — will he feel happy/sad/angry/afraid?

<u>Justification Question</u>: Why will he feel happy/sad/angry/afraid?

Angry Situations

Teacher: Describe the picture to the child and ask the child either to <u>say</u> how the person in the story feels, or to <u>point</u> to one of the emotion faces below.

Picture 37: Neil scribbles over Claire's picture and spoils it.

<u>Emotion Question</u>: How will Claire feel when Neil spoils her picture?
prompt — will she feel happy/sad/angry/afraid?

<u>Justification Question</u>: Why will she feel happy/sad/angry/afraid?

Teacher: Describe the picture to the child and ask the child either to <u>say</u> how the person in the story feels, or to <u>point</u> to one of the emotion faces below.

Picture 38: Melanie pushes Angela's tower. It falls over.

<u>Emotion Question</u>: How will Angela feel when Melanie pushes her tower over? *prompt — will she feel happy/sad/angry/afraid?*

<u>Justification Question</u>: Why will she feel happy/sad/angry/afraid?

Teacher: Describe the picture to the child and ask the child either to <u>say</u> how the person in the story feels, or to <u>point</u> to one of the emotion faces below.

Picture 39: Elaine kicks David's bat. It breaks in half.

<u>Emotion Question</u>: How will David feel when Elaine kicks his bat?
prompt — will he feel happy/sad/angry/afraid?

<u>Justification Question</u>: Why will he feel happy/sad/angry/afraid?

Teacher: Describe the picture to the child and ask the child either to <u>say</u> how the person in the story feels, or to <u>point</u> to one of the emotion faces below.

Picture 40: Malcolm jumps on Peter's toy car. It is broken.

<u>Emotion Question</u>: How will Peter feel when Malcolm jumps on his car?
prompt — will he feel happy/sad/angry/afraid?

<u>Justification Question</u>: Why will he feel happy/sad/angry/afraid?

Teacher: Describe the picture to the child and ask the child either to <u>say</u> how the person in the story feels, or to <u>point</u> to one of the emotion faces below.

Picture 41: Mary snatches William's lollipop. He cannot get it.

<u>Emotion Question</u>: How will William feel when Mary snatches his lollipop?
prompt — will he feel happy/sad/angry/afraid?

<u>Justification Question</u>: Why will he feel happy/sad/angry/afraid?

Teacher: Describe the picture to the child and ask the child either to <u>say</u> how the person in the story feels, or to <u>point</u> to one of the emotion faces below.

Picture 42: Bill takes Gavin's ball. Gavin cannot reach it.

<u>Emotion Question</u>: How will Gavin feel when Bill takes his ball?
prompt — will he feel happy/sad/angry/afraid?

<u>Justification Question</u>: Why will he feel happy/sad/angry/afraid?

Teacher: Describe the picture to the child and ask the child either to <u>say</u> how the person in the story feels, or to <u>point</u> to one of the emotion faces below.

Picture 43: Glenn takes Jacky's pen. Jacky cannot finish her picture.

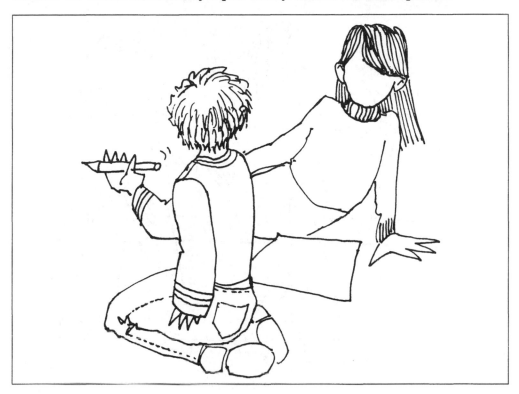

<u>Emotion Question</u>: How will Jacky feel when Glenn takes her pen?
prompt — will she feel happy/sad/angry/afraid?

<u>Justification Question</u>: Why will she feel happy/sad/angry/afraid?

Teacher: Describe the picture to the child and ask the child either to <u>say</u> how the person in the story feels, or to <u>point</u> to one of the emotion faces below.

Picture 44: Debbie snatches Carol's teddy and runs away with it.

<u>Emotion Question</u>: How will Carol feel when Debbie snatches her teddy?
prompt — will she feel happy/sad/angry/afraid?

<u>Justification Question</u>: Why will she feel happy/sad/angry/afraid?

Teacher: Describe the picture to the child and ask the child either to <u>say</u> how the person in the story feels, or to <u>point</u> to one of the emotion faces below.

Picture 45: Philip pushes Eddie over. Eddie cannot win the race.

<u>Emotion Question</u>: How will Eddie feel when Philip pushes him over?
prompt — will he feel happy/sad/angry/afraid?

<u>Justification Question</u>: Why will he feel happy/sad/angry/afraid?

Teacher: Describe the picture to the child and ask the child either to <u>say</u> how the person in the story feels, or to <u>point</u> to one of the emotion faces below.

Picture 46: Terry stops Alice from getting into the house.

<u>Emotion Question</u>: How will Alice feel when Eddie stops her getting into the house? *prompt — will she feel happy/sad/angry/afraid?*

<u>Justification Question</u>: Why will she feel happy/sad/angry/afraid?

Teacher: Describe the picture to the child and ask the child either to <u>say</u> how the person in the story feels, or to <u>point</u> to one of the emotion faces below.

Picture 47: Mummy says, "No more toys. It's time for bed."

<u>Emotion Question</u>: How will Ted feel when mummy says no more toys?
prompt — will she feel happy/sad/angry/afraid?

<u>Justification Question</u>: Why will she feel happy/sad/angry/afraid?

Teacher: Describe the picture to the child and ask the child either to <u>say</u> how the person in the story feels, or to <u>point</u> to one of the emotion faces below.

Picture 48: It's raining. Mummy won't let Lizzie play outside.

<u>Emotion Question</u>: How will Lizzie feel when mummy won't let her play outside? *prompt — will she feel happy/sad/angry/afraid?*

<u>Justification Question</u>: Why will she feel happy/sad/angry/afraid?

LEVEL 4. IDENTIFYING "DESIRE-BASED" EMOTIONS

These are the emotions caused by a person's desire being fulfilled or unfulfilled. At this level the child should be able to identify a character's feelings (either happy or sad) according to whether his or her wishes are fulfilled or not.

Materials and assessment procedures

A set of pictures revealing different facial expressions in a variety of emotional situations. The child needs to interpret the social and emotional context of the picture and predict what the emotional expression of the characters in it will be.
    The situations indicate **SADNESS OR HAPPINESS.**

Establishing a baseline

To assess desire-based emotion, pick four stories from the scenarios indicated below (two from Group A, and two from B). After you have described both pictures in the story, simply ask the child "How does *x* feel? happy or sad?' as suggested below.

Desire (Example 16A): Jennifer wants cake for tea.

Situation: Jennifer's daddy gives her cake for tea.

Picture One. **Look, this is Jennifer. This little picture tells us what Jennifer wants. Jennifer wants cake for tea.**

Picture Two. **Look, Jennifer's daddy has given her cake for tea.**

Desire Question: **What did Jennifer want?**

PROMPT: Look, this tells us what she wants. *Point to the small desire picture that is inset into Picture One.* **What did Jennifer want?**

> Emotion Question: **How will Jennifer feel when her daddy gives her cake for tea? Can you point to one of the faces?**
>
> **PROMPT: Will she feel happy or sad?** (Remember to vary the word order). *Point to each of the faces in turn.*
>
> **Let's see how Jennifer feels.** *Let the child point to the emotion face.*
>
> **Look,** if no answer or incorrect, prompt: **Jennifer is happy.**
>
> Why Question: **Why is she happy?**

If the child fails to predict the correct emotion on one or more stories out of the four selected then begin teaching at this level.

Teaching procedures

The tasks here test the child's ability to predict a character's emotion (happy/sad) depending on whether a wish is fulfilled or not. The teacher takes the child through the scene depicted on the first picture (illustrating what the character wants). Then s/he describes the scene on the next picture (illustrating what actually happens).

 The teacher then asks what the character wants, and how s/he will feel, prompting with the two possible alternatives (happy/sad). The child points to a face.

 Again, if the response is correct the teacher reinforces this and strengthens the child's understanding by asking "Why is he happy/sad etc. If the response is incorrect, the correct answer is provided, as is the reason for the character feeling this way.

> *Example of a desire-based emotion story (Desire fulfilled; Example 13A)*
> *Katie wants to catch a fish! Katie catches a big fish in the sea.*
> Picture One. **Look, this is Katie. This picture tells us what Katie wants. Katie wants to catch a fish.**
> Picture Two. **Look Katie catches a big fish in the sea.**
>
> Desire Question: **What did Katie want?**
>
> Emotion Question: **How will Katie feel when she catches the fish?**
> **PROMPT: Will she feel, happy or sad?**
> *Point to each of the faces in turn.*

Let's see how Katie feels. *The child can point to the face.*
Look, Katie is happy.

Why Question: **Why is she happy?**

Teaching
Emotion Question: For an incorrect response.
Let's have a look and see how Katie feels.
Look, Katie is happy. *Point to Katie's face.*
She is happy because she catches a fish. *Point to the fish.*
Katie is happy because she catches a fish. *Point to Katie.*

General teaching principle

Whether correct or incorrect, the child is always provided with the general principle underlying that emotion.

When you get something you want you feel happy.
If you don't get what you want you feel sad.

Figure 2.4 Nos 1–24
Pictures and procedures used in identifying "desired-based" emotions

Desire-based Happiness

Teacher: Tell the child the desire of the story character and then describe the story outcome. Check that the child understands the desire of the story character before asking the child either to <u>say</u> how the person in the story feels, or to <u>point</u> to one of the emotion faces below.

This is Eric. This picture tells us what Eric wants.
Desire 1A: Eric wants to go on the train.

Outcome 1A: Eric and his daddy are going on the train.

<u>Desire Question</u>: What does Eric want?
prompt — look, this picture tells you what Eric wants.

<u>Emotion Question</u>: How will Eric feel when he goes on the train?
prompt — will he feel happy/sad?

<u>Justification Question</u>: Why will he feel happy/sad?

Teacher: Tell the child the desire of the story character and then describe the story outcome. Check that the child understands the desire of the story character before asking the child either to <u>say</u> how the person in the story feels, or to <u>point</u> to one of the emotion faces below.

This is Tracy. This picture tells us what Tracy wants.
Desire 2A: Tracy wants an apple.

Outcome 2A: Mummy gives Tracy an apple for lunch.

<u>Desire Question</u>: What does Tracy want?
prompt — look, this picture tells you what Tracy wants.

<u>Emotion Question</u>: How will Tracy feel when her mummy gives her the apple?
prompt — will she feel happy/sad?

<u>Justification Question</u>: Why will she feel happy/sad?

Teacher: Tell the child the desire of the story character and then describe the story outcome. Check that the child understands the desire of the story character before asking the child either to <u>say</u> how the person in the story feels, or to <u>point</u> to one of the emotion faces below.

This is Toby. This picture tells us what Toby wants.
Desire 3A: Toby wants some hot chocolate.

Outcome 3A: At bedtime daddy makes Toby some hot chocolate.

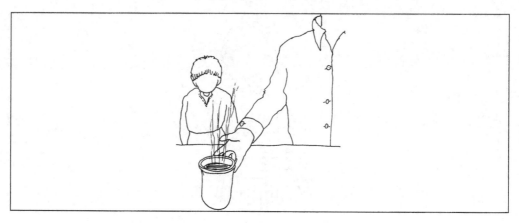

<u>Desire Question</u>: What does Toby want?
prompt — look, this picture tells you what Toby wants.

<u>Emotion Question</u>: How will Toby feel
when daddy makes him hot chocolate?
prompt — will he feel happy/sad?

<u>Justification Question</u>: Why will he feel
happy/sad?

Teacher: Tell the child the desire of the story character and then describe the story outcome. Check that the child understands the desire of the story character before asking the child either to <u>say</u> how the person in the story feels, or to <u>point</u> to one of the emotion faces below.

This is Claire. This picture tells us what Claire wants.
Desire 4A: Claire wants to see some pigs.

Outcome 4A: Claire's mum takes her to see some pigs.

<u>Desire Question</u>: What does Claire want?
prompt — look, this picture tells you what Claire wants.

<u>Emotion Question</u>: How will Claire feel when mummy takes her to see some pigs?
prompt — will she feel happy/sad?

<u>Justification Question</u>: Why will she feel happy/sad?

Teacher: Tell the child the desire of the story character and then describe the story outcome. Check that the child understands the desire of the story character before asking the child either to <u>say</u> how the person in the story feels, or to <u>point</u> to one of the emotion faces below.

This is George. This picture tells us what George wants.
Desire 5A: George wants some sweets.

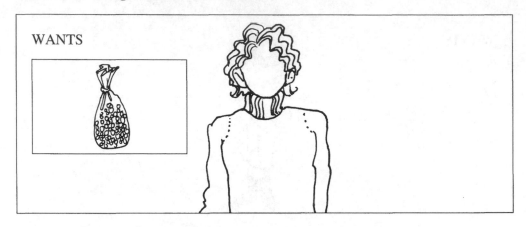

Outcome 5A: Lucy has bought George a packet of sweets.

<u>Desire Question</u>: What does George want?
prompt — look, this picture tells you what George wants.

<u>Emotion Question</u>: How will George feel when Lucy buys him a packet of sweets?
prompt — will he feel happy/sad?

<u>Justification Question</u>: Why will he feel happy/sad?

Teacher: Tell the child the desire of the story character and then describe the story outcome. Check that the child understands the desire of the story character before asking the child either to <u>say</u> how the person in the story feels, or to <u>point</u> to one of the emotion faces below.

This is Luke. This picture tells us what Luke wants.
Desire 6A: Luke wants to sail the boat.

Outcome 6A: Luke's daddy says "Let's sail the boat!"

<u>Desire Question</u>: What does Luke want?
prompt — look, this picture tells you what Luke wants.

<u>Emotion Question</u>: How will Luke feel when daddy <u>says</u> "Let's sail the boat!"
prompt — will he feel happy/sad?

<u>Justification Question</u>: Why will he feel happy/sad?

Teacher: Tell the child the desire of the story character and then describe the story outcome. Check that the child understands the desire of the story character before asking the child either to <u>say</u> how the person in the story feels, or to <u>point</u> to one of the emotion faces below.

This is Brian. This picture tells us what Brian wants.
Desire 7A: Brian wants to go the swimming pool.

Outcome 7A: Brian's sister takes him to the swimming pool.

<u>Desire Question</u>: What does Brian want?
prompt — look, this picture tells you what Brian wants.

<u>Emotion Question</u>: How will Brian feel when his sister takes him to the swimming pool?
prompt — will he feel happy/sad?

<u>Justification Question</u>: Why will he feel happy/sad?

Teacher: Tell the child the desire of the story character and then describe the story outcome. Check that the child understands the desire of the story character before asking the child either to <u>say</u> how the person in the story feels, or to <u>point</u> to one of the emotion faces below.

This is Jill. This picture tells us what Jill wants.
Desire 8A: Jill wants to fly the kite.

Outcome 8A: Brenda gives Jill the kite to fly.

<u>Desire Question</u>: What does Jill want?
prompt — look, this picture tells you what Jill wants.

<u>Emotion Question</u>: How will Jill feel when Brenda gives her the kite to fly?
prompt — will she feel happy/sad?

<u>Justification Question</u>: Why will she feel happy/sad?

Teacher: Tell the child the desire of the story character and then describe the story outcome. Check that the child understands the desire of the story character before asking the child either to <u>say</u> how the person in the story feels, or to <u>point</u> to one of the emotion faces below.

This is Jean. This picture tells us what Jean wants.
Desire 9A: Jean wants to go horse-riding.

Outcome 9A: Jean's mum takes her to horse-riding school.

<u>Desire Question</u>: What does Jean want?
prompt — look, this picture tells you what Jean wants.

<u>Emotion Question</u>: How will Jean feel when mum takes her to horse-riding school?
prompt — will she feel happy/sad?

<u>Justification Question</u>: Why will she feel happy/sad?

Teacher: Tell the child the desire of the story character and then describe the story outcome. Check that the child understands the desire of the story character before asking the child either to <u>say</u> how the person in the story feels, or to <u>point</u> to one of the emotion faces below.

This is Pat. This picture tells us what Pat wants.
Desire 10A: Pat wants an umbrella.

WANTS

Outcome 10A: Pat's mummy buys her an umbrella.

<u>Desire Question</u>: What does Pat want?
prompt — look, this picture tells you what Pat wants.

<u>Emotion Question</u>: How will Pat feel when mummy buys her an umbrella?
prompt — will she feel happy/sad?

<u>Justification Question</u>: Why will she feel happy/sad?

Teacher: Tell the child the desire of the story character and then describe the story outcome. Check that the child understands the desire of the story character before asking the child either to <u>say</u> how the person in the story feels, or to <u>point</u> to one of the emotion faces below.

This is Adrian. This picture tells us what Adrian wants.
Desire 11A: Adrian wants a car book.

Outcome 11A: Adrian's mummy has bought him a car book.

<u>Desire Question</u>: What does Adrian want?
prompt — look, this picture tells you what Adrian wants.

<u>Emotion Question</u>: How will Adrian feel when mummy buys him a car book?
prompt — will he feel happy/sad?

<u>Justification Question</u>: Why will he feel happy/sad?

Teacher: Tell the child the desire of the story character and then describe the story outcome. Check that the child understands the desire of the story character before asking the child either to <u>say</u> how the person in the story feels, or to <u>point</u> to one of the emotion faces below.

This is Paul. This picture tells us what Paul wants.
Desire 12A: Paul wants to go down the slide.

Outcome 12A: Ann pushes Paul down the slide.

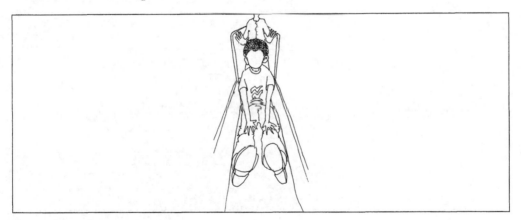

<u>Desire Question</u>: What does Paul want?
prompt — look, this picture tells you what Paul wants.

<u>Emotion Question</u>: How will Paul feel when Ann pushes him down the slide?
prompt — will he feel happy/sad?

<u>Justification Question</u>: Why will he feel happy/sad?

Teacher: Tell the child the desire of the story character and then describe the story outcome. Check that the child understands the desire of the story character before asking the child either to <u>say</u> how the person in the story feels, or to <u>point</u> to one of the emotion faces below.

This is Katie. This picture tells us what Katie wants.
Desire 13A: Katie wants to catch a fish.

Outcome 13A: Katie has caught a big fish in the sea.

<u>Desire Question</u>: What does Katie want?
prompt — look, this picture tells you what Katie wants.

<u>Emotion Question</u>: How will Katie feel when she catches a big fish in the sea?
prompt — will she feel happy/sad?

<u>Justification Question</u>: Why will she feel happy/sad?

Teacher: Tell the child the desire of the story character and then describe the story outcome. Check that the child understands the desire of the story character before asking the child either to <u>say</u> how the person in the story feels, or to <u>point</u> to one of the emotion faces below.

This is Sam. This picture tells us what Sam wants.
Desire 14A: Sam wants some paints.

Outcome 14A: Sam's mum has bought him a tin of paints.

<u>Desire Question</u>: What does Sam want?
prompt — look, this picture tells you what Sam wants.

<u>Emotion Question</u>: How will Sam feel when mum buys him a tin of paints?
prompt — will he feel happy/sad?

<u>Justification Question</u>: Why will he feel happy/sad?

Teacher: Tell the child the desire of the story character and then describe the story outcome. Check that the child understands the desire of the story character before asking the child either to <u>say</u> how the person in the story feels, or to <u>point</u> to one of the emotion faces below.

This is Billy. This picture tells us what Billy wants.
Desire 15A: Billy wants to go on the merry-go-round.

Outcome 15A: Billy is going round and round on the horse.

<u>Desire Question</u>: What does Billy want?
prompt — look, this picture tells you what Billy wants.

<u>Emotion Question</u>: How will Billy feel when the horse goes round and round?
prompt — will he feel happy/sad?

<u>Justification Question</u>: Why will he feel happy/sad?

Teacher: Tell the child the desire of the story character and then describe the story outcome. Check that the child understands the desire of the story character before asking the child either to <u>say</u> how the person in the story feels, or to <u>point</u> to one of the emotion faces below.

This is Jennifer. This picture tells us what Jennifer wants.
Desire 16A: Jennifer wants cake for tea.

Outcome 16A: Jennifer's daddy gives her cake for tea.

<u>Desire Question</u>: What does Jennifer want?
prompt — look, this picture tells you what Jennifer wants.

<u>Emotion Question</u>: How will Jennifer feel when daddy gives her cake for tea?
prompt — will she feel happy/sad?

<u>Justification Question</u>: Why will she feel happy/sad?

Teacher: Tell the child the desire of the story character and then describe the story outcome. Check that the child understands the desire of the story character before asking the child either to <u>say</u> how the person in the story feels, or to <u>point</u> to one of the emotion faces below.

This is Thomas. This picture tells us what Thomas wants.
Desire 17A: Thomas wants to see clowns at the circus.

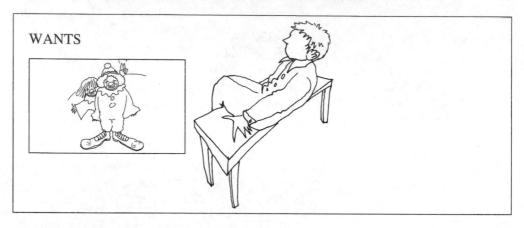

Outcome 17A: Thomas sees clowns at the circus.

<u>Desire Question</u>: What does Thomas want?
prompt — look, this picture tells you what Thomas wants.

<u>Emotion Question</u>: How will Thomas feel when he sees clowns at the circus?
prompt — will he feel happy/sad?

<u>Justification Question</u>: Why will he feel happy/sad?

Teacher: Tell the child the desire of the story character and then describe the story outcome. Check that the child understands the desire of the story character before asking the child either to <u>say</u> how the person in the story feels, or to <u>point</u> to one of the emotion faces below.

This is Alan. This picture tells us what Alan wants.
Desire 18A: Alan wants a chocolate ice-cream.

Outcome 18A: Alan's daddy buys him a chocolate ice-cream.

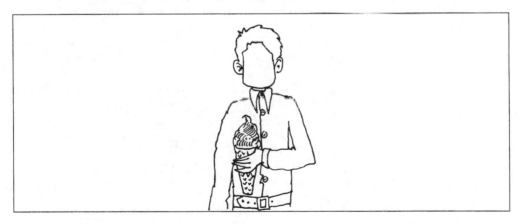

<u>Desire Question</u>: What does Alan want?
prompt — look, this picture tells you what Alan wants.

<u>Emotion Question</u>: How will Alan feel when daddy buys him a chocolate ice-cream?
prompt — will he feel happy/sad?

<u>Justification Question</u>: Why will he feel happy/sad?

Teacher: Tell the child the desire of the story character and then describe the story outcome. Check that the child understands the desire of the story character before asking the child either to <u>say</u> how the person in the story feels, or to <u>point</u> to one of the emotion faces below.

This is Jane. This picture tells us what Jane wants.
Desire 19A: Jane wants Elizabeth to push her on the swing.

Outcome 19A: Elizabeth pushes Jane up and down on the swing.

<u>Desire Question</u>: What does Jane want?
prompt — look, this picture tells you what Jane wants.

<u>Emotion Question</u>: How will Jane feel when Elizabeth pushes her on the swing?
prompt — will she feel happy/sad?

<u>Justification Question</u>: Why will she feel happy/sad?

Teacher: Tell the child the desire of the story character and then describe the story outcome. Check that the child understands the desire of the story character before asking the child either to <u>say</u> how the person in the story feels, or to <u>point</u> to one of the emotion faces below.

This is Josie. This picture tells us what Josie wants.
Desire 20A: Josie wants Nigel to go to the party.

Outcome 20A: Josie and Nigel go to the birthday party.

<u>Desire Question</u>: What does Josie want?
prompt — look, this picture tells you what Josie wants.

<u>Emotion Question</u>: How will Josie feel when Nigel goes to the party?
prompt — will she feel happy/sad?

<u>Justification Question</u>: Why will she feel happy/sad?

Teacher: Tell the child the desire of the story character and then describe the story outcome. Check that the child understands the desire of the story character before asking the child either to <u>say</u> how the person in the story feels, or to <u>point</u> to one of the emotion faces below.

This is Daniel. This picture tells us what Daniel wants.
Desire 21A: Daniel wants to ride his bike to the shops.

Outcome 21A: Daniel's mummy asks him to ride to the shops.

<u>Desire Question</u>: What does Daniel want?
prompt — look, this picture tells you what Daniel wants.

<u>Emotion Question</u>: How will Daniel feel when mummy asks him to ride to the shops?
prompt — will he feel happy/sad?

<u>Justification Question</u>: Why will he feel happy/sad?

Teacher: Tell the child the desire of the story character and then describe the story outcome. Check that the child understands the desire of the story character before asking the child either to <u>say</u> how the person in the story feels, or to <u>point</u> to one of the emotion faces below.

This is Tina. This picture tells us what Tina wants.
Desire 22A: Tina wants a flower picture.

Outcome 22A: Tina's sister buys her a flower picture.

<u>Desire Question</u>: What does Tina want?
prompt — look, this picture tells you what Tina wants.

<u>Emotion Question</u>: How will Tina feel when her sister buys her a flower picture?
prompt — will she feel happy/sad?

<u>Justification Question</u>: Why will she feel happy/sad?

Teacher: Tell the child the desire of the story character and then describe the story outcome. Check that the child understands the desire of the story character before asking the child either to <u>say</u> how the person in the story feels, or to <u>point</u> to one of the emotion faces below.

This is Matthew. This picture tells us what Matthew wants.
Desire 23A: Matthew wants a toy aeroplane.

Outcome 23A: Matthew's brother gives him a toy aeroplane.

<u>Desire Question</u>: What does Matthew want?
prompt — look, this picture tells you what Matthew wants.

<u>Emotion Question</u>: How will Matthew feel when his brother gives him a toy aeroplane?
prompt — will he feel happy/sad?

<u>Justification Question</u>: Why will he feel happy/sad?

Teacher: Tell the child the desire of the story character and then describe the story outcome. Check that the child understands the desire of the story character before asking the child either to <u>say</u> how the person in the story feels, or to <u>point</u> to one of the emotion faces below.

This is Betty. This picture tells us what Betty wants.
Desire 24A: Betty wants a teddy for her birthday.

Outcome 24A: Betty's grandma gives Betty a teddy for her birthday.

<u>Desire Question</u>: What does Betty want?
prompt — look, this picture tells you what Betty wants.

<u>Emotion Question</u>: How will Betty feel when grandma gives her a teddy for her birthday?
prompt — will she feel happy/sad?

<u>Justification Question</u>: Why will she feel happy/sad?

Desire-based Sadness

Teacher: Tell the child the desire of the story character and then describe the story outcome. Check that the child understands the desire of the story character before asking the child either to <u>say</u> how the person in the story feels, or to <u>point</u> to one of the emotion faces below.

This is Eric. This picture tells us what Eric wants.
Desire 1B: Eric wants to go in the car.

Outcome 1B: Eric and his daddy are going on the train.

<u>Desire Question</u>: What does Eric want?
prompt — look, this picture tells you what Eric wants.

<u>Emotion Question</u>: How will Eric feel when he goes on the train?
prompt — will he feel happy/sad?

<u>Justification Question</u>: Why will he feel happy/sad?

Teacher: Tell the child the desire of the story character and then describe the story outcome. Check that the child understands the desire of the story character before asking the child either to <u>say</u> how the person in the story feels, or to <u>point</u> to one of the emotion faces below.

This is Tracy. This picture tells us what Tracy wants.
Desire 2B: Tracy wants a banana.

Outcome 2B: Mummy gives Tracy an apple for lunch.

<u>Desire Question</u>: What does Tracy want?
prompt — look, this picture tells you what Tracy wants.

<u>Emotion Question</u>: How will Tracy feel when mummy gives her an apple for lunch?
prompt — will she feel happy/sad?

<u>Justification Question</u>: Why will she feel happy/sad?

Teacher: Tell the child the desire of the story character and then describe the story outcome. Check that the child understands the desire of the story character before asking the child either to <u>say</u> how the person in the story feels, or to <u>point</u> to one of the emotion faces below.

This is Toby. This picture tells us what Toby wants.
Desire 3B: Toby wants some orange juice.

Outcome 3B: At bedtime daddy makes Toby some hot chocolate.

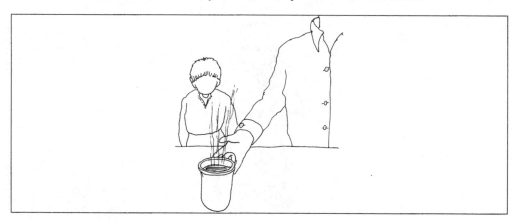

<u>Desire Question</u>: What does Toby want?
prompt — look, this picture tells you what Toby wants.

<u>Emotion Question</u>: How will Toby feel when daddy makes him hot chocolate?
prompt — will he feel happy/sad?

<u>Justification Question</u>: Why will he feel happy/sad?

Teacher: Tell the child the desire of the story character and then describe the story outcome. Check that the child understands the desire of the story character before asking the child either to <u>say</u> how the person in the story feels, or to <u>point</u> to one of the emotion faces below.

This is Claire. This picture tells us what Claire wants.
Desire 4B: Claire wants to see some lambs.

Outcome 4B: Claire's mum takes her to see some pigs.

<u>Desire Question</u>: What does Claire want.
prompt — look, this picture tells you what Claire wants.

<u>Emotion Question</u>: How will Claire feel when mummy takes her to see some pigs?
prompt — will she feel happy/sad?

<u>Justification Question</u>: Why will she feel happy/sad?

Teacher: Tell the child the desire of the story character and then describe the story outcome. Check that the child understands the desire of the story character before asking the child either to <u>say</u> how the person in the story feels, or to <u>point</u> to one of the emotion faces below.

This is George. This picture tells us what George wants.
Desire 5B: George wants some crisps.

Outcome 5B: Lucy has bought George a packet of sweets.

<u>Desire Question</u>: What does George want?
prompt — look, this picture tells you what George wants.

<u>Emotion Question</u>: How will George feel when Lucy buys him a packet of sweets?
prompt — will he feel happy/sad?

<u>Justification Question</u>: Why will he feel happy/sad?

Teacher: Tell the child the desire of the story character and then describe the story outcome. Check that the child understands the desire of the story character before asking the child either to <u>say</u> how the person in the story feels, or to <u>point</u> to one of the emotion faces below.

This is Luke. This picture tells us what Luke wants.
Desire 6B: Luke wants to feed the ducks.

Outcome 6B: Luke's daddy says "Let's sail the boat!"

<u>Desire Question</u>: What does Luke want?
prompt — look, this picture tells you what Luke wants.

<u>Emotion Question</u>: How will Luke feel when daddy says 'Let's sail the boat!"
prompt — will he feel happy/sad?

<u>Justification Question</u>: Why will he feel happy/sad?

Teacher: Tell the child the desire of the story character and then describe the story outcome. Check that the child understands the desire of the story character before asking the child either to <u>say</u> how the person in the story feels, or to <u>point</u> to one of the emotion faces below.

This is Brian. This picture tells us what Brian wants.
Desire 7B: Brian wants to go to the seaside.

Outcome 7B: Brian's sister takes him to the swimming pool.

<u>Desire Question</u>: What does Brian want?
prompt — look, this picture tells you what Brian wants.

<u>Emotion Question</u>: How will Brian feel when his sister takes him to the swimming pool?
prompt — will he feel happy/sad?

<u>Justification Question</u>: Why will he feel happy/sad?

Teacher: Tell the child the desire of the story character and then describe the story outcome. Check that the child understands the desire of the story character before asking the child either to <u>say</u> how the person in the story feels, or to <u>point</u> to one of the emotion faces below.

This is Jill. This picture tells us what Jill wants.
Desire 8B: Jill wants to go on the swing.

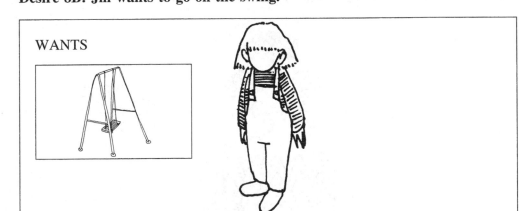

WANTS

Outcome 8B: Brenda gives Jill the kite to fly.

<u>Desire Question</u>: What does Jill want?
prompt — look, this picture tells you what Jill wants.

<u>Emotion Question</u>: How will Jill feel when Brenda gives her the kite to fly?
prompt — will she feel happy/sad?

<u>Justification Question</u>: Why will she feel happy/sad?

Teacher: Tell the child the desire of the story character and then describe the story outcome. Check that the child understands the desire of the story character before asking the child either to <u>say</u> how the person in the story feels, or to <u>point</u> to one of the emotion faces below.

This is Jean. This picture tells us what Jean wants.
Desire 9B: Jean wants to go dancing.

Outcome 9B: Jean's mum takes her to horse-riding school.

<u>Desire Question</u>: What does Jean want?
prompt — look, this picture tells you what Jean wants.

<u>Emotion Question</u>: How will Jean feel when her mum takes her to horse-riding school?
prompt — will she feel happy/sad?

<u>Justification Question</u>: Why will she feel happy/sad?

Teacher: Tell the child the desire of the story character and then describe the story outcome. Check that the child understands the desire of the story character before asking the child either to <u>say</u> how the person in the story feels, or to <u>point</u> to one of the emotion faces below.

This is Pat. This picture tells us what Pat wants.
Desire 10B: Pat wants a rain hat.

WANTS

Outcome 10B: Pat's mummy buys her an umbrella.

<u>Desire Question</u>: What does Pat want?
prompt — look, this picture tells you what Pat wants.

<u>Emotion Question</u>: How will Pat feel when mummy buys her an umbrella?
prompt — will she feel happy/sad?

<u>Justification Question</u>: Why will she feel happy/sad?

Teacher: Tell the child the desire of the story character and then describe the story outcome. Check that the child understands the desire of the story character before asking the child either to <u>say</u> how the person in the story feels, or to <u>point</u> to one of the emotion faces below.

This is Adrian. This picture tells us what Adrian wants.
Desire 11B: Adrian wants a train book.

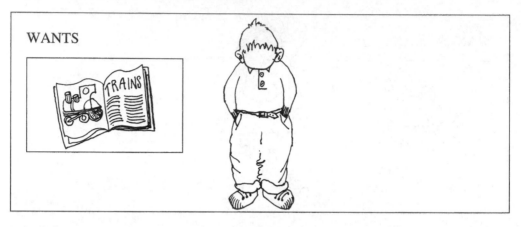

Outcome 11B: Adrian's mummy has bought him a car book.

<u>Desire Question</u>: What does Adrian want?
prompt — look, this picture tells you what Adrian wants.

<u>Emotion Question</u>: How will Adrian feel when mummy buys him a car book?
prompt — will he feel happy/sad?

<u>Justification Question</u>: Why will he feel happy/sad?

Teacher: Tell the child the desire of the story character and then describe the story outcome. Check that the child understands the desire of the story character before asking the child either to <u>say</u> how the person in the story feels, or to <u>point</u> to one of the emotion faces below.

This is Paul. This picture tells us what Paul wants.
Desire 12B: Paul wants to stay at the top of the slide.

Outcome 12B: Ann pushes Paul down the slide.

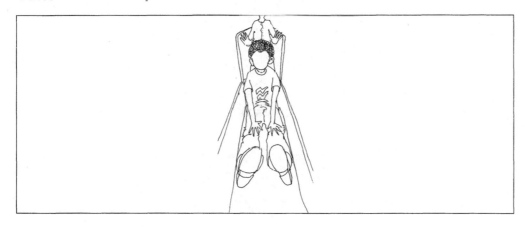

<u>Desire Question</u>: What does Paul want?
prompt — look, this picture tells you what Paul wants.

<u>Emotion Question</u>: How will Paul feel when Ann pushes him down the slide?
prompt — will he feel happy/sad?

<u>Justification Question</u>: Why will he feel happy/sad?

Teacher: Tell the child the desire of the story character and then describe the story outcome. Check that the child understands the desire of the story character before asking the child either to <u>say</u> how the person in the story feels, or to <u>point</u> to one of the emotion faces below.

This is Katie. This picture tells us what Katie wants.
Desire 13B: Katie wants to catch a crab.

Outcome 13B: Katie has caught a big fish in the sea.

<u>Desire Question</u>: What does Katie want?
prompt — look, this picture tells you what Katie wants.

<u>Emotion Question</u>: How will Katie feel when she catches a big fish in the sea?
prompt — will she feel happy/sad?

<u>Justification Question</u>: Why will she feel happy/sad?

Teacher: Tell the child the desire of the story character and then describe the story outcome. Check that the child understands the desire of the story character before asking the child either to <u>say</u> how the person in the story feels, or to <u>point</u> to one of the emotion faces below.

This is Sam. This picture tells us what Sam wants.
Desire 14B: Sam wants a toy car.

Outcome 14B: Sam's mum has bought him a tin of paints.

<u>Desire Question</u>: What does Sam want?
prompt — look, this picture tells you what Sam wants.

<u>Emotion Question</u>: How will Sam feel when mum buys him a tin of paints?
prompt — will he feel happy/sad?

<u>Justification Question</u>: Why will he feel happy/sad?

Teacher: Tell the child the desire of the story character and then describe the story outcome. Check that the child understands the desire of the story character before asking the child either to <u>say</u> how the person in the story feels, or to <u>point</u> to one of the emotion faces below.

This is Billy. This picture tells us what Billy wants.
Desire 15B: Billy wants to go on the helter-skelter.

Outcome 15B: Billy is going round and round on the horse.

<u>Desire Question</u>: What does Billy want?
prompt — look, this picture tells you what Billy wants.

<u>Emotion Question</u>: How will Billy feel
when the horse goes round and round?
prompt — will he feel happy/sad?

<u>Justification Question</u>: Why will he feel
happy/sad?

Teacher: Tell the child the desire of the story character and then describe the story outcome. Check that the child understands the desire of the story character before asking the child either to __say__ how the person in the story feels, or to __point__ to one of the emotion faces below.

This is Jennifer. This picture tells us what Jennifer wants.
Desire 16B: Jennifer wants jelly for tea.

Outcome 16B: Jennifer's daddy gives her cake for tea.

Desire Question: What does Jennifer want?
prompt — look, this picture tells you what Jennifer wants.

Emotion Question: How will Jennifer feel when daddy gives her cake for tea?
prompt — will she feel happy/sad?

Justification Question: Why will she feel happy/sad?

Teacher: Tell the child the desire of the story character and then describe the story outcome. Check that the child understands the desire of the story character before asking the child either to <u>say</u> how the person in the story feels, or to <u>point</u> to one of the emotion faces below.

This is Thomas. This picture tells us what Thomas wants.
Desire 17B: Thomas wants to see lions at the circus.

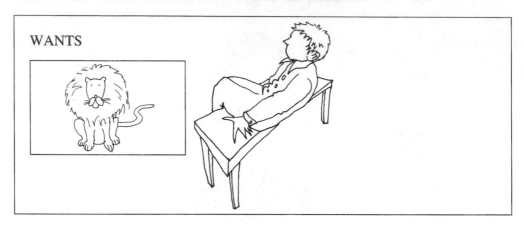

Outcome 17B: Thomas sees clowns at the circus.

<u>Desire Question</u>: What does Thomas want?
prompt — look, this picture tells you what Thomas wants.

<u>Emotion Question</u>: How will Thomas feel when he sees clowns at the circus?
prompt — will he feel happy/sad?

<u>Justification Question</u>: Why will he feel happy/sad?

Teacher: Tell the child the desire of the story character and then describe the story outcome. Check that the child understands the desire of the story character before asking the child either to <u>say</u> how the person in the story feels, or to <u>point</u> to one of the emotion faces below.

This is Alan. This picture tells us what Alan wants.
Desire 18B: Alan wants a strawberry ice-cream.

Outcome 18B: Alan's daddy buys him a chocolate ice-cream.

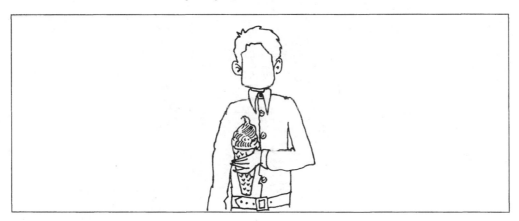

<u>Desire Question</u>: What does Alan want?
prompt — look, this picture tells you what Alan wants.

<u>Emotion Question</u>: How will Alan feel when daddy buys him a chocolate ice-cream?
prompt — will he feel happy/sad?

<u>Justification Question</u>: Why will he feel happy/sad?

Teacher: Tell the child the desire of the story character and then describe the story outcome. Check that the child understands the desire of the story character before asking the child either to <u>say</u> how the person in the story feels, or to <u>point</u> to one of the emotion faces below.

This is Jane. This picture tells us what Jane wants.
Desire 19B: Jane wants to go on the see-saw.

Outcome 19B: Elizabeth pushes Jane up and down on the swing.

<u>Desire Question</u>: What does Jane want?
prompt — look, this picture tells you what Jane wants.

<u>Emotion Question</u>: How will Jane feel when Elizabeth pushes her on the swing?
prompt — will she feel happy/sad?

<u>Justification Question</u>: Why will she feel happy/sad?

Teacher: Tell the child the desire of the story character and then describe the story outcome. Check that the child understands the desire of the story character before asking the child either to <u>say</u> how the person in the story feels, or to <u>point</u> to one of the emotion faces below.

This is Josie. This picture tells us what Josie wants.
Desire 20B: Josie wants Nigel to stay at home.

Outcome 20B: Josie and Nigel go to the birthday party.

<u>Desire Question</u>: What does Josie want?
prompt — look, this picture tells you what Josie wants.

<u>Emotion Question</u>: How will Josie feel when Nigel goes to the party?
prompt — will she feel happy/sad?

<u>Justification Question</u>: Why will she feel happy/sad?

Teacher: Tell the child the desire of the story character and then describe the story outcome. Check that the child understands the desire of the story character before asking the child either to <u>say</u> how the person in the story feels, or to <u>point</u> to one of the emotion faces below.

This is Daniel. This picture tells us what Daniel wants.
Desire 21B: Daniel wants to ride his bike to the park.

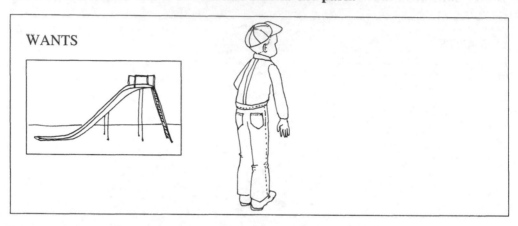

Outcome 21B: Daniel's mummy asks him to ride to the shops.

<u>Desire Question</u>: What does Daniel want?
prompt — look, this picture tells you what Daniel wants.

<u>Emotion Question</u>: How will Daniel feel when mummy asks him to ride to the shops?
prompt — will he feel happy/sad?

<u>Justification Question</u>: Why will he feel happy/sad?

Teacher: Tell the child the desire of the story character and then describe the story outcome. Check that the child understands the desire of the story character before asking the child either to <u>say</u> how the person in the story feels, or to <u>point</u> to one of the emotion faces below.

This is Tina. This picture tells us what Tina wants.
Desire 22B: Tina wants a kitten picture.

Outcome 22B: Tina's sister buys her a flower picture.

<u>Desire Question</u>: What does Tina want?
prompt — look, this picture tells you what Tina wants.

<u>Emotion Question</u>: How will Tina feel when her sister buys her a flower picture?
prompt — will she feel happy/sad?

<u>Justification Question</u>: Why will she feel happy/sad?

Teacher: Tell the child the desire of the story character and then describe the story outcome. Check that the child understands the desire of the story character before asking the child either to <u>say</u> how the person in the story feels, or to <u>point</u> to one of the emotion faces below.

This is Matthew. This picture tells us what Matthew wants.
Desire 23B: Matthew wants a toy train.

Outcome 23B: Matthew's brother gives him a toy aeroplane.

<u>Desire Question</u>: What does Matthew want?
prompt — look, this picture tells you what Matthew wants.

<u>Emotion Question</u>: How will Matthew feel when his brother gives him a toy aeroplane?
prompt — will he feel happy/sad?

<u>Justification Question</u>: Why will he feel happy/sad?

Teacher: Tell the child the desire of the story character and then describe the story outcome. Check that the child understands the desire of the story character before asking the child either to <u>say</u> how the person in the story feels, or to <u>point</u> to one of the emotion faces below.

This is Betty. This picture tells us what Betty wants.
Desire 24B: Betty wants a doll for her birthday.

Outcome 24B: Betty's grandma gives Betty a teddy for her birthday.

<u>Desire Question</u>: What does Betty want?
prompt — look, this picture tells you what Betty wants.

<u>Emotion Question</u>: How will Betty feel when grandma gives her a teddy for her birthday?
prompt — will she feel happy/sad?

<u>Justification Question</u>: Why will she feel happy/sad?

LEVEL 5. IDENTIFYING "BELIEF-BASED" EMOTIONS

These are emotions caused by what someone thinks is the case, even if what they think conflicts with reality. The child is required to follow a sequence of three pictures and to predict the emotion that a cartoon character will experience according to whether they *believe* their desires have been satisfied or not.

Materials and assessment procedures

There are black-and-white pictures for each of the belief-based emotion stories. The first picture shows the reality of the situation. The second picture shows the character. His/her desire and belief are represented by two small black-and-white pictures which are inset into the larger picture. The final picture shows the story outcome as revealed to the character.

In both the second and third pictures the character's face is blank and the child has to point to the correct facial expression below. Two black-and-white pictures are used for children to indicate their choice of emotion.

The child needs to interpret the social/emotional context of the picture and predict what the emotional expression of the characters in it will be. The situations indicate **SADNESS OR HAPPINESS**. The emotions felt depend on whether beliefs and desires coincide or conflict in some way as the following examples indicate.

1. True belief/ (See Example 1A) fulfilled desire)			
Reality Jennifer's daddy buys her cake.	**Desire** Jennifer wants cake for tea.	**Belief** Jennifer thinks there is cake for tea.	Jennifer will feel . . .
Daddy gives her cake for tea.		**Emotion: Happy**	**Outcome: Happy**

2. True belief/ (See Example 5B) unfulfilled desire			
Reality The rope on Joanna's swing is broken. Joanna cannot play on her swing.	**Desire** Joanna wants to play on her swing	**Belief** Joanna thinks her swing is broken. **Emotion: Sad**	Joanna will feel . . . **Outcome: Sad**

3. Fulfilled desire/ (See Example 5C) false belief			
Reality Adrian's mummy buys him a book about cars. Adrian's mummy gives him a book about cars.	**Desire** Adrian wants a book about cars.	**Belief** Adrian doesn't know that his mummy has bought a book about cars. He thinks she's bought a train book. **Emotion: Sad**	Adrian will feel . . . **Outcome: Happy**

4. Unfulfilled (See Example 5D) desire/false belief			
Reality Mummy has an apple for Tracy's lunch. Mummy gives Tracy the apple for lunch.	**Desire** Tracy wants a banana.	**Belief** Tracy doesn't know about the apple, she thinks mummy has a banana. **Emotion: Happy**	Tracy will feel . . . **Outcome: Sad**

Illustrations of all the pictures used to assess belief based emotions are provided in Figure 2.5. below.

Establishing a baseline

Stories in this section require two emotion judgements. In the first emotion judgement story the character is unaware of the story outcome. The judgement is, therefore, based solely on what the story character *wants* and *believes* to be true about a situation.

A belief about a situation can be either true or false, and a desire can be either fulfilled or unfulfilled. In the 12 stories in Section A, the story character has a true belief about a situation and his or her desire is fulfilled. In Section B, 12 stories consist of a character who has a true belief but whose desire is not fulfilled. In Section C, the character's belief about a situation is false and his or her desire is fulfilled. In Section D, the character's belief about a situation is false and his or her desire is unfulfilled.

The second emotion judgement is based on how the character feels on his or her discovery of the story outcome.

First, describe the actual situation to the child (top picture). Then show the child the story character's desire and belief (second picture). Check that the child understands the desire and the belief of the character. For the first emotion judgement ask the child either to *say* how the character feels or to *point* to one of the emotion faces, in the light of the character's desire and belief. For the second emotion judgement ask the child to indicate how the character in the story feels about the outcome (third picture).

To assess belief-based emotion, pick four stories from those illustrated below (one from each section A, B, C and D). After you have described both pictures in the story, ask the child "What does *x* want?"; "What does he think s/he will get?"; "How will *x* feel?"; "Why will s/he feel (happy or sad)?" as indicated below.

Assessing Belief-based emotion — (Example 2B). Situation: Tina's sister buys her a picture of some flowers

Desire: Tina wants a picture of a kitten.
Belief: Tina thinks her sister has a flower picture.

Picture One. **Look, this is Tina's sister; she's got a flower picture for Tina.**
Picture Two: **This is Tina. This little picture tells us what Tina wants and this picture tells us what Tina thinks.**
Tina wants a kitten picture, but she thinks her sister has bought a flower picture.
Point to the pictures appropriately.

Desire Question: **What does Tina want?**

PROMPT: Look, this picture tells us what Tina wants. *Point to the desire picture that is inset into the second picture.* **What does she want? She wants a . . .**

Belief Question: **What does Tina think her sister has got for her?**

PROMPT: Look, this picture tells us what Tina thinks. *Point to the belief picture that is inset into the second picture.*
What does Tina think her sister has for her? She thinks she's got . . .

Belief-based Emotion Question (1): **How will Tina feel when she thinks her sister has a flower picture for her? Can you point to one of the faces?**

PROMPT: Will she feel happy or sad? *Point to each of the faces in turn.*

Justification Question (1): **Why will Tina feel** [child's response]?
Look, let's see how Tina feels. *The child can point to the faces at the bottom of the page.*
Look, Tina is sad.

Picture Three. **Look, Tina's sister gives her the flower picture**
Outcome-Emotion Question (2): **How will Tina feel when her sister gives her the flower picture?**

If the child fails one or more of the belief-based emotion stories from the four selected begin teaching at this level.

Teaching procedures

The teacher goes through the pictures (indicating the character's wishes and then his or her beliefs) prompting the child to say what the character thinks, what s/he wants, what s/he feels and why. If the responses are correct the teacher reinforces these and strengthens the child's understanding by asking "Why does he feel happy/sad etc. If the responses are incorrect, the correct answers are provided, as are the reasons for the character feeling this way.

A Belief-based emotion story (Example 1, Section B): **Situation: Matthew's brother has a toy aeroplane for him.**
Desire: Matthew wants a toy train.
Belief: Matthew thinks his brother has bought a train.

Picture One. **Look, Matthew's brother has a toy aeroplane for him.**
Picture Two. **This is Matthew. This little picture tells us what Matthew wants and this picture tells us what Matthew thinks. Matthew wants a toy train. Matthew doesn't know about the aeroplane. He thinks his brother has bought a train.**

Desire Question: **What does Matthew want?**
PROMPT: Look, this picture tells us what Matthew wants.
Point to the desire picture that is inset into the second picture.
What does he want? He wants a . . .

Belief Question: **What does Matthew think his brother has for him?**
PROMPT: Look, this picture tells us what Matthew thinks.
Point to the belief picture that is inset into the second picture.
What does Matthew think his brother has for him? He thinks he's got . . .

Emotion Question: **How will Matthew feel when he thinks his brother has a train for him? Can you point to one of the faces?**
PROMPT: Will he feel happy or sad?
Point to each of the faces in turn.

Look, let's see how Matthew feels. *The child can point to the face.*
Look, Matthew is happy.

Justification Question: **Why is he happy?**

General teaching principle

Whether correct or incorrect the child is always provided with the general principle underlying that emotion.

If you want something to happen and it does, you will feel happy.

If you want to do something but you can't, you will feel sad.

If someone thinks they have got what they want, they will feel happy, even if they are not going to get what they wanted.

If someone thinks they have not got what they want, they will feel sad, even if they are going to get what they wanted.

Figure 2.5 Nos 1A–12D
Pictures and procedures used in identifying "belief-based" emotions

Section A: True belief and fulfilled desire

Example 1A.
Actual Situation: Jennifer's daddy buys her cake for tea.

This is Jennifer. This picture tells us what Jennifer wants.
Desire: Jennifer wants cake for tea.
This picture tells us what Jennifer thinks.
Belief: Jennifer thinks there is cake for tea.

Desire Question: What does Jennifer want?
prompt — look, this picture tells us what Jennifer wants.
Belief Question: What does Jennifer think?
prompt — look, this picture tells us what Jennifer thinks.
Emotion Question: Jennifer wants cake. Jennifer thinks there is cake for tea. How does Jennifer feel?
prompt — does she feel happy/sad?
Justification Question: Why will she feel happy/sad?

Outcome: Jennifer's daddy gives her cake for tea.

<u>Desire Question</u>: What does Jennifer want?
prompt — look, this picture tells us what Jennifer wants.

<u>Emotion Question</u>: How will Jennifer feel when daddy gives her cake for tea?
prompt — will she feel happy/sad?

<u>Justification Question</u>: Why will she fell happy/sad?

Example 2A.
Actual Situation: Sam's mum buys him some paints.

This is Sam. This picture tells us what Sam wants.
Desire: Sam wants some paints.
This picture tells us what Sam thinks.
Belief: Sam thinks mum has bought him some paints.

Desire Question: What does Sam want?
prompt — look, this picture tells us what Sam wants.
Belief Question: What does Sam think?
prompt — look, this picture tells us what Sam thinks.
Emotion Question: Sam wants some paints. Sam thinks mum has bought him some
paints. How does Sam feel?
prompt — does he feel happy/sad?
Justification Question: Why does he
feel happy/sad?

Outcome: Sam's mum gives him the tin of paints.

<u>Desire Question</u>: What does Sam want?
prompt — look, this picture tells us what Sam wants.

<u>Emotion Question</u>: How will Sam feel when mum gives him the tin of paints?
prompt — will he feel happy/sad?

<u>Justification Question</u>: Why will he feel happy/sad?

Example 3A.
Actual Situation: Betty's grandma buys Betty a teddy for her birthday.

This is Betty. This picture tells us what Betty wants.
Desire: Betty wants a teddy for her birthday.
This picture tells us what Betty thinks.
Belief: Betty thinks grandma has bought her a teddy.

Desire Question: What does Betty want?
prompt — look, this picture tells us what Betty wants.
Belief Question: What does Betty think?
prompt — look, this picture tells us what Betty thinks.
Emotion Question: Betty wants a teddy. Betty thinks grandma has bought her a
teddy. How does Betty feel?
prompt — does she feel happy/sad?
Justification Question: Why will she
feel happy/sad?

Outcome: Betty's grandma gives her the teddy for her birthday.

<u>Desire Question</u>: What does Betty want?
prompt — look, this picture tells us what Betty wants.

<u>Emotion Question</u>: How will Betty feel when grandma gives her the teddy for her birthday?
prompt — will she feel happy/sad?

<u>Justification Question</u>: Why will she feel happy/sad?

Example 4A.
Actual Situation: Elizabeth is going to push Jane on the swing.

This is Jane. This picture tells us what Jane wants.
Desire: Jane wants Elizabeth to push her.
This picture tells us what Jane thinks.
Belief: Jane thinks Elizabeth will push her.

Desire Question: What does Jane want?
prompt — look, this picture tells us what Jane wants.
Belief Question: What does Jane think?
prompt — look, this picture tells us what Jane thinks.
Emotion Question: Jane wants Elizabeth to push her. Jane thinks Elizabeth will push her. How does Jane feel?
prompt — does she feel happy/sad?
Justification Question: Why does she feel happy/sad?

Outcome: Elizabeth pushes Jane up and down on the swing.

<u>Desire Question</u>: What does Jane want?
prompt — look, this picture tells us what Jane wants.

<u>Emotion Question</u>: How will Jane feel if Elizabeth pushes her up and down on the swing?
prompt — will she feel happy/sad?

<u>Justification Question</u>: Why will she feel happy/sad?

Example 5A.
Actual Situation: Nigel is going to the birthday party.

This is Josie. This picture tells us what Josie wants.
Desire: Josie wants Nigel to go to the party.
This picture tells us what Josie thinks.
Belief: Josie thinks Nigel is going to the party.

Desire Question: What does Josie want?
prompt — look, this picture tells us what Josie wants.
Belief Question: What does Josie think?
prompt — look, this picture tells us what Josie thinks.
Emotion Question: Josie wants Nigel to go to the party. Josie thinks Nigel is going
to the party. How does Josie feel?
prompt — does she feel happy/sad?
Justification Question: Why does she
feel happy/sad?

Outcome: Josie and Nigel go to the birthday party.

<u>Desire Question</u>: What does Josie want?
prompt — look, this picture tells us what Josie wants.

<u>Emotion Question</u>: How will Josie feel when Nigel goes to the birthday party?
prompt — will she feel happy/sad?

<u>Justification Question</u>: Why will she feel happy/sad?

Example 6A.
Actual Situation: Alan's daddy buys him a chocolate ice-cream.

This is Alan. This picture tells us what Alan wants.
Desire: Alan wants a chocolate ice-cream.
This picture tells us what Alan thinks.
Belief: Alan thinks daddy has bought him a chocolate ice-cream.

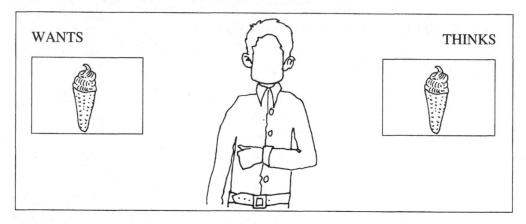

<u>Desire Question</u>: What does Alan want?
prompt — look, this picture tells us what Alan wants.
<u>Belief Question</u>: What does Alan think?
prompt — look, this picture tells us what Alan thinks.
<u>Emotion Question</u>: Alan wants a chocolate ice-cream. Alan thinks daddy has bought him a chocolate ice-cream. How does Alan feel?

prompt — does he feel happy/sad?
<u>Justification Question</u>: Why does he feel happy/sad?

Outcome: Alan's daddy gives him the chocolate ice-cream.

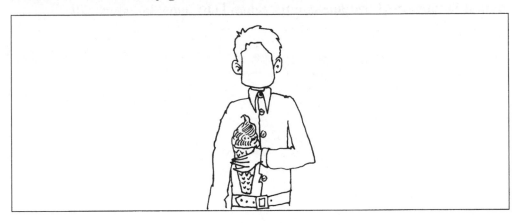

Desire Question: What does Alan want?
prompt — look, this picture tells us what Alan wants.

Emotion Question: How will Alan feel when daddy gives him the chocolate ice-cream?
prompt — will he feel happy/sad?

Justification Question: Why will he feel happy/sad?

Example 7A.
Actual Situation: At bedtime daddy makes Toby some hot chocolate.

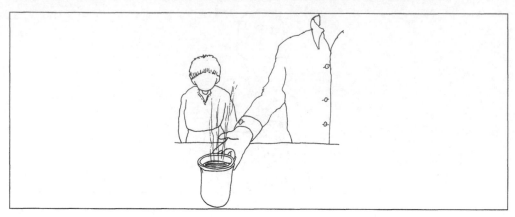

This is Toby. This picture tells us what Toby wants.
Desire: Toby wants some hot chocolate.
This picture tells us what Toby thinks.
Belief: Toby thinks daddy has hot chocolate for him.

Desire Question: What does Toby want?
prompt — look, this picture tells us what Toby wants.
Belief Question: What does Toby think?
prompt — look, this picture tells us what Toby thinks.
Emotion Question: Toby wants hot chocolate. Toby thinks his daddy has hot chocolate for him. How does Toby feel?
prompt — does he feel happy/sad?
Justification Question: Why does he
feel happy/sad?

Outcome: Daddy gives Toby the hot chocolate at bedtime.

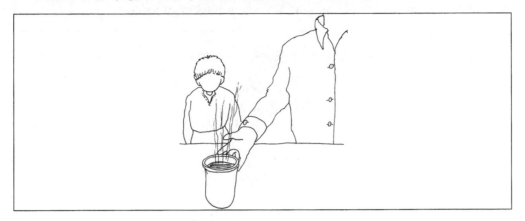

<u>Desire Question</u>: What does Toby want?
prompt — look, this picture tells us what Toby wants.

<u>Emotion Question</u>: How will Toby feel when his daddy gives him hot chocolate at bedtime?
prompt — will he feel happy/sad?

<u>Justification Question</u>: Why will he feel happy/sad?

Example 8A.
Actual Situation: Lucy has bought George a packet of sweets.

This is George. This picture tells us what George wants.
Desire: George wants some sweets.
This picture tells us what George thinks.
Belief: George thinks Lucy has some sweets for him.

<u>Desire Question</u>: What does George want?
prompt — look, this picture tells us what George wants.
<u>Belief Question</u>: What does George think?
prompt — look, this picture tells us what George thinks.
<u>Emotion Question</u>: George wants some sweets. George thinks Lucy has some sweets
for him. How does George feel?
prompt — does he feel happy/sad?
<u>Justification Question</u>: Why does he
feel happy/sad?

Outcome: Lucy gives George the packet of sweets.

<u>Desire Question</u>: What does George want?
prompt — look, this picture tells us what George wants.

<u>Emotion Question</u>: How will George feel when Lucy gives him the packet of sweets?
prompt — will he feel happy/sad?

<u>Justification Question</u>: Why will he feel happy/sad?

Example 9A.
Actual Situation: Brenda has a kite for Jill to fly.

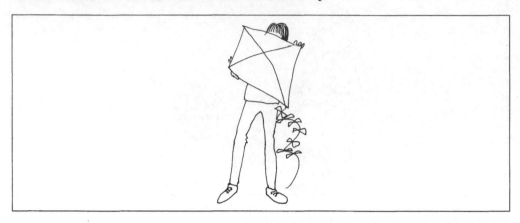

This is Jill. This picture tells us what Jill wants.
Desire: Jill wants to fly the kite.
This picture tells us what Jill thinks.
Belief: Jill thinks Brenda will give her the kite to fly.

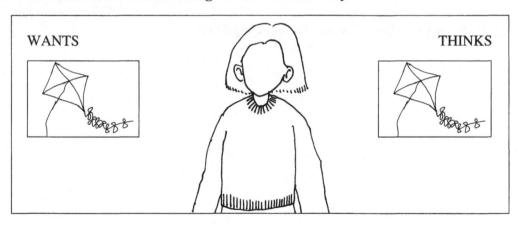

Desire Question: What does Jill want?
prompt — look, this picture tells us what Jill wants.
Belief Question: What does Jill think?
prompt — look, this picture tells us what Jill thinks.
Emotion Question: Jill wants to fly the kite. Jill thinks Brenda will give her the kite
to fly.
prompt — does she feel happy/sad?
Justification Question: Why does she
feel happy/sad?

Outcome: Brenda gives Jill the kite to fly.

<u>Desire Question</u>: What does Jill want?
prompt — look, this picture tells us what Jill wants.

<u>Emotion Question</u>: How will Jill feel when Brenda gives her the kite to fly?
prompt — will she feel happy/sad?

<u>Justification Question</u>: Why will she feel happy/sad?

Example 10A.
Actual Situation: Brian's sister is taking him to the swimming pool.

This is Brian. This picture tells us what Brian wants.
Desire: Brian wants to go to the swimming pool.
This picture tells us what Brian thinks.
Belief: Brian thinks they are going to the pool.

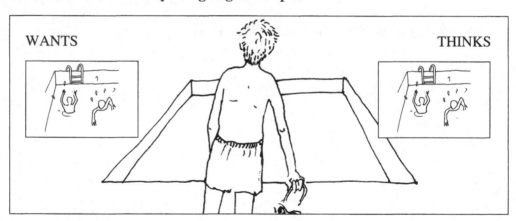

<u>Desire Question</u>: What does Brian want?
prompt — look, this picture tells us what Brian wants.
<u>Belief Question</u>: What does Brian think?
prompt — look, this picture tells us what Brian thinks.
<u>Emotion Question</u>: Brian wants to go to the swimming pool. Brian thinks they are
going to the pool. How does Brian feel?
prompt — does he feel happy/sad?
<u>Justification Question</u>: Why does he
feel happy/sad?

Outcome: Brian's sister takes him to the swimming pool.

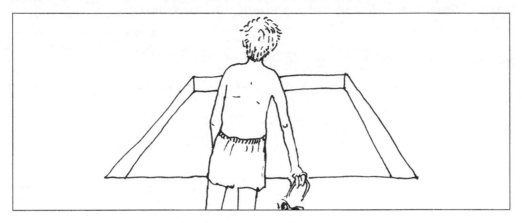

<u>Desire Question</u>: What does Brian want?
prompt — look, this picture tells us what Brian wants.

<u>Emotion Question</u>: How will Brian feel when Brenda takes him to the swimming pool?
prompt — will he feel happy/sad?

<u>Justification Question</u>: Why will he feel happy/sad?

Example 11A.
Actual Situation: Eric and daddy are going on the train.

This is Eric. This picture tells us what Eric wants.
Desire: Eric wants to go on the train.
This picture tells us what Eric thinks.
Belief: Eric thinks daddy is taking him on the train.

Desire Question: What does Eric want?
prompt — look, this picture tells us what Eric wants.
Belief Question: What does Eric think?
prompt — look, this picture tells us what Eric thinks.
Emotion Question: Eric wants to go on the train. Eric thinks daddy is taking him on the train. How does Eric feel?
prompt — does he feel happy/sad?
Justification Question: Why does he feel happy/sad?

Outcome: Eric and daddy go on the train.

<u>Desire Question</u>: What does Eric want?
prompt — look, this picture tells us what Eric wants.

<u>Emotion Question</u>: How will Eric feel when him and daddy go on the train?
prompt — will he feel happy/sad?

<u>Justification Question</u>: Why will he feel happy/sad?

Example 12A.
Actual Situation: Luke's daddy is going to sail the boat.

This is Luke. This picture tells us what Luke wants.
Desire: Luke wants to sail the boat.
This picture tells us what Luke thinks.
Belief: Luke thinks daddy will sail the boat.

Desire Question: What does Luke want?
prompt — look, this picture tells us what Luke wants.
Belief Question: What does Luke think?
prompt — look, this picture tells us what Luke thinks.
Emotion Question: Luke wants to sail the boat. Luke thinks his daddy will sail the boat. How does Luke feel?
prompt — does he feel happy/sad?
Justification Question: Why does he feel happy/sad?

Outcome: Luke's daddy says "let's sail the boat."

<u>Desire Question</u>: What does Luke want?
prompt — look, this picture tells us what Luke wants.

<u>Emotion Question</u>: How will Luke feel when daddy says "Let's sail the boat"?
prompt — will he feel happy/sad?

<u>Justification Question</u>: Why will he feel happy/sad?

Section B: True belief and unfulfilled desire
Example 1B.
Actual Situation: Matthew's brother has a toy aeroplane for him.

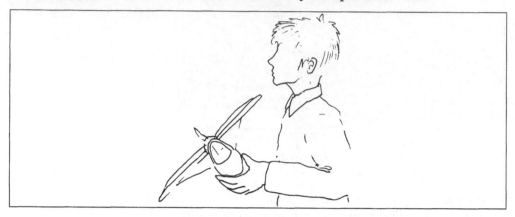

This is Matthew. This picture tells us what Matthew wants.
Desire: Matthew wants a toy train.
This picture tells us what Matthew thinks.
Belief: Matthew thinks his brother has an aeroplane for him.

WANTS   THINKS

<u>Desire Question</u>: What does Matthew want?
prompt — look, this picture tells us what Matthew wants.
<u>Belief Question</u>: What does Matthew think?
prompt — look, this picture tells us what Matthew thinks.
<u>Emotion Question</u>: Matthew wants a toy train. Matthew thinks his brother has an aeroplane. How does Matthew feel?
prompt — does he feel happy/sad?
<u>Justification Question</u>: Why does he feel happy/sad?

Outcome: Matthew's brother gives him the toy aeroplane.

<u>Desire Question</u>: What does Matthew want?
prompt — look, this picture tells us what Matthew wants.

<u>Emotion Question</u>: How will Matthew feel when his brother gives him the toy aeroplane?
prompt — will he feel happy/sad?

<u>Justification Question</u>: Why will he feel happy/sad?

Example 2B.
Actual Situation: Tina's sister buys her a picture of some flowers.

This is Tina. This picture tells us what Tina wants.
Desire: Tina wants a kitten picture.
This picture tells us what Tina thinks.
Belief: Tina thinks her sister has a flower picture.

<u>Desire Question</u>: What does Tina want?
prompt — look, this picture tells us what Tina wants.
<u>Belief Question</u>: What does Tina think?
prompt — look, this picture tells us what Tina thinks.
<u>Emotion Question</u>: Tina wants a kitten picture. Tina thinks her sister has a flower
picture. How does Tina feel?
prompt — does she feel happy/sad?
<u>Justification Question</u>: Why does she
feel happy/sad?

Outcome: Tina's sister gives her the flower picture.

<u>Desire Question</u>: What does Tina want?
prompt — look, this picture tells us what Tina wants.

<u>Emotion Question</u>: How will Tina feel when her sister gives her the flower picture?
prompt — will she feel happy/sad?

<u>Justification Question</u>: Why will she feel happy/sad?

Example 3B.
Actual Situation: The clowns will be at the circus.

This is Thomas. This picture tells us what Thomas wants.
Desire: Thomas wants to see the lions.
This picture tells us what Thomas thinks.
Belief: Thomas thinks there are clowns at the circus.

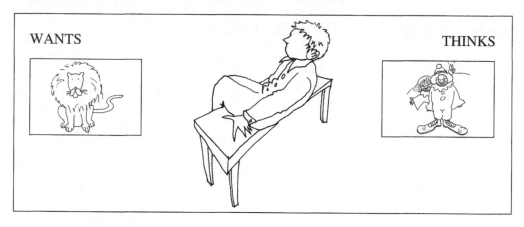

<u>Desire Question</u>: What does Thomas want?
prompt — look, this picture tells us what Thomas wants.
<u>Belief Question</u>: What does Thomas think?
prompt — look, this picture tells us what Thomas thinks.
<u>Emotion Question</u>: Thomas wants to see the lions. Thomas thinks he will see clowns
at the circus. How does Thomas feel?
prompt — does he feel happy/sad?
<u>Justification Question</u>: Why does he
feel happy/sad?

Outcome: Thomas sees the clowns at the circus.

<u>Desire Question</u>: What does Thomas want?
prompt — look, this picture tells us what Thomas wants.

<u>Emotion Question</u>: How will Thomas feel when he sees the clowns at the circus?
prompt — will he feel happy/sad?

<u>Justification Question</u>: Why will he feel happy/sad?

Example 4B.
Actual Situation: It's time for Adam's granddad to go home.

This is Adam. This picture tells us what Adam wants.
Desire: Adam wants his granddad to stay.
This picture tells us what Adam thinks.
Belief: Adam thinks his granddad is going home.

WANTS   THINKS

<u>Desire Question</u>: What does Adam want?
prompt — look, this picture tells us what Adam wants.
<u>Belief Question</u>: What does Adam think?
prompt — look, this picture tells us what Adam thinks.
<u>Emotion Question</u>: Adam wants his granddad to stay. Adam thinks his granddad is
going home. How does Adam feel?
prompt — does he feel happy/sad?
<u>Justification Question</u>: Why does he
feel happy/sad?

Outcome: Adam's granddad says goodbye and goes home.

Desire Question: What does Adam want?
prompt — look, this picture tells us what Adam wants.

Emotion Question: How will Adam feel when his granddad says goodbye and goes home?
prompt — will he feel happy/sad?

Justification Question: Why will he feel happy/sad?

Example 5B.
Actual Situation: The rope on Joanne's swing is broken.

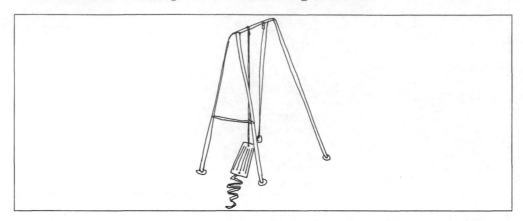

This is Joanne. This picture tells us what Joanne wants.
Desire: Joanne wants to play on her swing.
This picture tells us what Joanne thinks.
Belief: Joanne thinks her swing is broken.

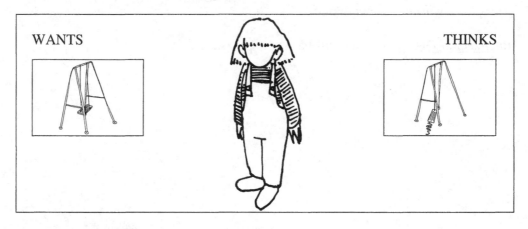

<u>Desire Question</u>: What does Joanne want?
prompt — look, this picture tells us what Joanne wants.
<u>Belief Question</u>: What does Joanne think?
prompt — look, this picture tells us what Joanne thinks.
<u>Emotion Question</u>: Joanne wants to play on her swing. Joanne thinks her swing is broken. How does Joanne feel?
prompt — does she feel happy/sad?
<u>Justification Question</u>: Why does she feel happy/sad?

Outcome: Joanne cannot play on her swing. It's broken.

<u>Desire Question</u>: What does Joanne want?
prompt — look, this picture tells us what Joanne wants.

<u>Emotion Question</u>: How will Joanne feel when her swing is broken?
prompt — will she feel happy/sad?

<u>Justification Question</u>: Why will she feel happy/sad?

Example 6B.
Actual Situation: The handles have fallen off Marie's bike.

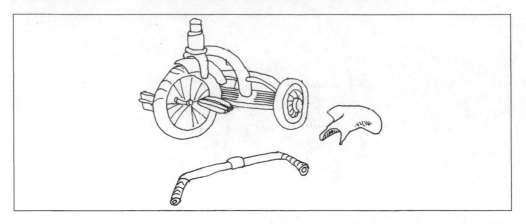

This is Marie. This picture tells us what Marie wants.
Desire: Marie wants to play on her bike.
This picture tells us what Marie thinks.
Belief: Marie thinks her bike is broken.

Desire Question: What does Marie want?
prompt — look, this picture tells us what Marie wants.
Belief Question: What does Marie think?
prompt — look, this picture tells us what Marie thinks.
Emotion Question: Marie wants to play on her bike. Marie thinks her bike is broken. How does Marie feel?
prompt — does she feel happy/sad?
Justification Question: Why does she feel happy/sad

Outcome: Marie cannot play on her bike. It's broken.

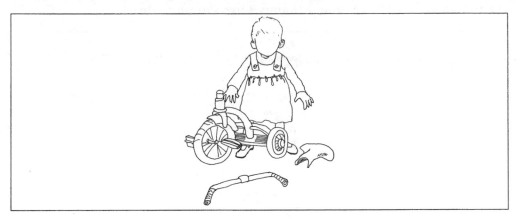

<u>Desire Question</u>: What does Marie want?
prompt — look, this picture tells us what Marie wants.

<u>Emotion Question</u>: How will Marie feel when her bike is broken?
prompt — will she feel happy/sad?

<u>Justification Question</u>: Why will she feel happy/sad?

Example 7B.
Actual Situation: It's raining. Mummy buys Pat an umbrella.

This is Pat. This picture tells us what Pat wants.
Desire: Pat wants a rain hat.
This picture tells us what Pat thinks.
Belief: Pat thinks mummy has bought her an umbrella.

Desire Question: What does Pat want?
prompt — look, this picture tells us what Pat wants.
Belief Question: What does Pat think?
prompt — look, this picture tells us what Pat thinks.
Emotion Question: Pat wants a rain hat. Pat thinks mummy has bought her an umbrella. How does Pat feel?
prompt — does she feel happy/sad?
Justification Question: Why does she feel happy/sad?

Outcome: Mummy gives Pat the umbrella to keep her dry.

<u>Desire Question</u>: What does Pat want?
prompt — look, this picture tells us what Pat wants.

<u>Emotion Question</u>: How will Pat feel when her mummy gives her the umbrella?
prompt — will she feel happy/sad?

<u>Justification Question</u>: Why will she feel happy/sad?

Example 8B.
Actual Situation: Adrian's mummy buys him a book about cars.

This is Adrian. This picture tells us what Adrian wants.
Desire: Adrian wants a book about trains.
This picture tells us what Adrian thinks.
Belief: Adrian thinks mummy has bought a car book.

<u>Desire Question</u>: What does Adrian want?
prompt — look, this picture tells us what Adrian wants.
<u>Belief Question</u>: What does Adrian think?
prompt — look, this picture tells us what Adrian thinks.
<u>Emotion Question</u>: Adrian wants a train book. Adrian thinks mummy has bought a car book. How does Adrian feel?
prompt — does he feel happy/sad?
<u>Justification Question</u>: Why does he feel happy/sad?

Outcome: Adrian's mummy gives him the book about cars.

<u>Desire Question</u>: What does Adrian want?
prompt — look, this picture tells us what Adrian wants.

<u>Emotion Question</u>: How will Adrian feel when mummy gives him the car book?
prompt — will he feel happy/sad?

<u>Justification Question</u>: Why will he feel happy/sad?

Example 9B.
Actual Situation: Mummy and Claire are going to see some pigs.

This is Claire. This picture tells us what Claire wants.
Desire: Claire wants to see some lambs.
This picture tells us what Claire thinks.
Belief: Claire thinks they will see some pigs.

Desire Question: What does Claire want?
prompt — look, this picture tells us what Claire wants.
Belief Question: What does Claire think?
prompt — look, this picture tells us what Claire thinks.
Emotion Question: Claire wants to see some lambs. Claire thinks they will see some pigs. How does Claire feel?
prompt — does she feel happy/sad?
Justification Question: Why does she feel happy/sad?

Outcome: Claire sees the pigs on the farm.

<u>Desire Question</u>: What does Claire want?
prompt — look, this picture tells us what Claire wants.

<u>Emotion Question</u>: How will Claire feel when she sees the pigs on the farm?
prompt — will she feel happy/sad?

<u>Justification Question</u>: Why will she feel happy/sad?

Example 10B.
Actual Situation: Mummy has an apple for Tracy's lunch.

This is Tracy. This picture tells us what Tracy wants.
Desire: Tracy wants a banana.
This picture tells us what Tracy thinks.
Belief: Tracy thinks mummy has an apple for her.

Desire Question: What does Tracy want?
prompt — look, this picture tells us what Tracy wants.
Belief Question: What does Tracy think?
prompt — look, this picture tells us what Tracy thinks.
Emotion Question: Tracy wants a banana. Tracy thinks mummy has an apple for
her. How does Tracy feel?
prompt — does she feel happy/sad?
Justification Question: Why does she
feel happy/sad?

Outcome: Mummy gives Tracy the apple for lunch.

<u>Desire Question</u>: What does Tracy want?
prompt — look, this picture tells us what Tracy wants.

<u>Emotion Question</u>: How will Tracy feel when mummy gives her the apple for lunch?
prompt — will she feel happy/sad?

<u>Justification Question</u>: Why will she feel happy/sad?

Example 11B.
Actual Situation: Jean's mum is taking her horse-riding.

This is Jean. This picture tells us what Jean wants.
Desire: Jean wants to go dancing.
This picture tells us what Jean thinks.
Belief: Jean thinks mum is taking her horse-riding.

WANTS   THINKS

Desire Question: What does Jean want?
prompt — look, this picture tells us what Jean wants.
Belief Question: What does Jean think?
prompt — look, this picture tells us what Jean thinks.
Emotion Question: Jean wants to go dancing. Jean thinks mum is taking her horse-riding. How does Jean feel?
prompt — does she feel happy/sad?
Justification Question: Why does she feel happy/sad?

Outcome: Jean's mum takes her horse-riding.

<u>Desire Question</u>: What does Jean want?
prompt — look, this picture tells us what Jean wants.

<u>Emotion Question</u>: How will Jean feel when mum takes her horse-riding?
prompt — will she feel happy/sad?

<u>Justification Question</u>: Why will she feel happy/sad?

Example 12B.
Actual Situation: Billy is going round and round on the horse.

This is Billy. This picture tells us what Billy wants.
Desire: Billy wants to go on the helter-skelter.
This picture tells us what Billy thinks.
Belief: Billy thinks the horse will not stop.

<u>Desire Question</u>: What does Billy want?
prompt — look, this picture tells us what Billy wants.
<u>Belief Question</u>: What does Billy think?
prompt — look, this picture tells us what Billy thinks.
<u>Emotion Question</u>: Billy wants to go on the helter-skelter. Billy thinks the horse
will not stop. How does Billy feel?
prompt — does he feel happy/sad?
<u>Justification Question</u>: Why does he
feel happy/sad?

Outcome: The horse keeps going round and round.

<u>Desire Question</u>: What does Billy want?
prompt — look, this picture tells us what Billy wants.

<u>Emotion Question</u>: How will Billy feel when the horse keeps going round and round?
prompt — will he feel happy/sad?

<u>Justification Question</u>: Why will he feel happy/sad?

Section C: False belief and fulfilled desire
Example 1C.
Actual Situation: Jennifer's daddy gives her cake for tea.

This is Jennifer. This picture tells us what Jennifer wants.
Desire: Jennifer wants cake.
This picture tells us what Jennifer thinks.
Belief: Jennifer doesn't know about the cake. She thinks there is jelly for tea.

Desire Question: What does Jennifer want?
prompt — look, this picture tells us what Jennifer wants.
Belief Question: What does Jennifer think?
prompt — look, this picture tells us what Jennifer thinks.
Emotion Question: Jennifer wants cake. Jennifer thinks there is jelly for tea. How does Jennifer feel?
prompt — does she feel happy/sad?
Justification Question: Why does she feel happy/sad?

Outcome: Jennifer's daddy gives her cake for tea.

<u>Desire Question</u>: What does Jennifer want?
prompt — look, this picture tells us what Jennifer wants.

<u>Emotion Question</u>: How will Jennifer feel when daddy gives her cake for tea?
prompt — will she feel happy/sad?

<u>Justification Question</u>: Why will she feel happy/sad?

Example 2C.
Actual Situation: Alan's daddy buys him a chocolate ice-cream.

This is Alan. This picture tells us what Alan wants.
Desire: Alan wants a chocolate ice-cream.
This picture tells us what Alan thinks.
Belief: Alan doesn't know about the chocolate ice-cream. He thinks daddy has a strawberry ice-cream.

<u>Desire Question</u>: What does Alan want?
prompt — look, this picture tells us what Alan wants.
<u>Belief Question</u>: What does Alan think?
prompt — look, this picture tells us what Alan thinks.
<u>Emotion Question</u>: Alan wants a chocolate ice-cream. Alan thinks daddy has a strawberry ice-cream. How does Alan feel?
prompt — does he feel happy/sad?
<u>Justification Question</u>: Why does he feel happy/sad?

Outcome: Alan's daddy gives him the chocolate ice-cream.

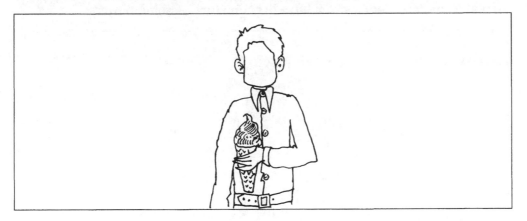

<u>Desire Question</u>: What does Alan want?
prompt — look, this picture tells us what Alan wants.

<u>Emotion Question</u>: How will Alan feel when daddy gives him the chocolate ice-cream?
prompt — will he feel happy/sad?

<u>Justification Question</u>: Why will he feel happy/sad?

Example 3C.
Actual Situation: Tina's sister buys her a picture of some flowers.

This is Tina. This picture tells us what Tina wants.
Desire: Tina wants a flower picture.
This picture tells us what Tina thinks.
Belief: Tina doesn't know about the flower picture. She thinks her sister has a kitten picture.

Desire Question: What does Tina want?
prompt — look, this picture tells us what Tina wants.
Belief Question: What does Tina think?
prompt — look, this picture tells us what Tina thinks.
Emotion Question: Tina wants a flower picture. Tina thinks her sister has a kitten picture. How does Tina feel?
prompt — does she feel happy/sad?
Justification Question: Why does she feel happy/sad?

Outcome: Tina's sister gives her a picture of some flowers.

<u>Desire Question</u>: What does Tina want?
prompt — look, this picture tells us what Tina wants.

<u>Emotion Question</u>: How will Tina feel when her sister gives her the flower picture?
prompt — will she feel happy/sad?

<u>Justification Question</u>: Why will she feel happy/sad?

Example 4C.
Actual Situation: Lucy buys George a packet of sweets.

This is George. This picture tells us what George wants.
Desire: George wants some sweets.
This picture tells us what George thinks.
Belief: George doesn't know about the sweets. He thinks Lucy has crisps for him.

Desire Question: What does George want?
prompt — look, this picture tells us what George wants.
Belief Question: What does George think?
prompt — look, this picture tells us what George thinks.
Emotion Question: George wants some sweets. George thinks Lucy has crisps for him. How does George feel?
prompt — does he feel happy/sad?
Justification Question: Why does he feel happy/sad?

Outcome: Lucy gives George the packet of sweets.

Desire Question: What does George want?
prompt — look, this picture tells us what George wants.

Emotion Question: How will George feel when Lucy gives him the packet of sweets?
prompt — will he feel happy/sad?

Justification Question: Why will he feel happy/sad?

Example 5C.
Actual Situation: Adrian's mummy buys him a book about cars.

This is Adrian. This picture tells us what Adrian wants.
Desire: Adrian wants a car book.
This picture tells us what Adrian thinks.
Belief: Adrian doesn't know about the car book. He thinks mummy has bought him a train book.

<u>Desire Question</u>: What does Adrian want?
prompt — look, this picture tells us what Adrian wants.
<u>Belief Question</u>: What does Adrian think?
prompt — look, this picture tells us what Adrian thinks.
<u>Emotion Question</u>: Adrian wants a car book. Adrian thinks mummy has bought him a train book. How does Adrian feel?
prompt — does he feel happy/sad?
<u>Justification Question</u>: Why does he feel happy/sad?

Outcome: Adrian's mummy gives him the book about cars.

<u>Desire Question</u>: What does Adrian want?
prompt — look, this picture tells us what Adrian wants.

<u>Emotion Question</u>: How will Adrian feel when mummy gives him the car book?
prompt — will he feel happy/sad?

<u>Justification Question</u>: Why will he feel happy/sad?

Example 6C.
Actual Situation: Eric and daddy are going on the train.

This is Eric. This picture tells us what Eric wants.
Desire: Eric wants to go on the train.
This picture tells us what Eric thinks.
Belief: Eric doesn't know about the train. He thinks they are going in the car.

<u>Desire Question</u>: What does Eric want?
prompt — look, this picture tells us what Eric wants.
<u>Belief Question</u>: What does Eric think?
prompt — look, this picture tells us what Eric thinks.
<u>Emotion Question</u>: Eric wants to go on the train. Eric thinks they are going in the car. How does Eric feel?
prompt — does he feel happy/sad?
<u>Justification Question</u>: Why does he feel happy/sad?

Outcome: Eric and daddy go on the train.

<u>Desire Question</u>: What does Eric want?
prompt — look, this picture tells us what Eric wants.

<u>Emotion Question</u>: How will Eric feel when him and daddy go on the train?
prompt — will he feel happy/sad?

<u>Justification Question</u>: Why will he feel happy/sad?

Example 7C.
Actual Situation: Claire's mum is taking her to see some pigs.

This is Claire. This picture tells us what Claire wants.
Desire: Claire wants to see some pigs.
This picture tells us what Claire thinks.
Belief: Claire doesn't know about the pigs. She thinks they will see some lambs.

<u>Desire Question</u>: What does Claire want?
prompt — look, this picture tells us what Claire wants.
<u>Belief Question</u>: What does Claire think?
prompt — look, this picture tells us what Claire thinks.
<u>Emotion Question</u>: Claire wants to see some pigs. Claire thinks they will see some lambs. How does Claire feel?
prompt — does she feel happy/sad?
<u>Justification Question</u>: Why does she feel happy/sad?

Outcome: Claire sees the pigs on the farm.

<u>Desire Question</u>: What does Claire want?
prompt — look, this picture tells us what Claire wants.

<u>Emotion Question</u>: How will Claire feel when she sees the pigs on the farm?
prompt — will she feel happy/sad?

<u>Justification Question</u>: Why will she feel happy/sad?

Example 8C.
Actual Situation: Nigel is going to the birthday party.

This is Josie. This picture tells us what Josie wants.
Desire: Josie wants Nigel to go to the party.
This picture tells us what Josie thinks.
Belief: Josie doesn't know Nigel is going. She thinks Nigel is staying at home.

Desire Question: What does Josie want?
prompt — look, this picture tells us what Josie wants.
Belief Question: What does Josie think?
prompt — look, this picture tells us what Josie thinks.
Emotion Question: Josie wants Nigel to go to the party. Josie thinks Nigel is staying at home. How does Josie feel?
prompt — does she feel happy/sad?
Justification Question: Why does she
feel happy/sad?

Outcome: Josie and Nigel go to the birthday party.

<u>Desire Question</u>: What does Josie want?
prompt — look, this picture tells us what Josie wants.

<u>Emotion Question</u>: How will Josie feel when her and Nigel go to the birthday party?
prompt — will she feel happy/sad?

<u>Justification Question</u>: Why will she feel happy/sad?

Example 9C.
Actual Situation: Sam's mum has bought him a tin of paints.

This is Sam. This picture tells us what Sam wants.
Desire: Sam wants some paints.
This picture tells us what Sam thinks.
Belief: Sam doesn't know about the paints. He thinks mum has bought him a toy car.

Desire Question: What does Sam want?
prompt — look, this picture tells us what Sam wants.
Belief Question: What does Sam think?
prompt — look, this picture tells us what Sam thinks.
Emotion Question: Sam wants some paints. Sam thinks mum has bought him a toy car. How does Sam feel?
prompt — does he feel happy/sad?
Justification Question: Why does he feel happy/sad?

Outcome: Sam's mum gives him the tin of paints.

<u>Desire Question</u>: What does Sam want?
prompt — look, this picture tells us what Sam wants.

<u>Emotion Question</u>: How will Sam feel when mum gives him the tin of paints?
prompt — will he feel happy/sad?

<u>Justification Question</u>: Why will he feel happy/sad?

Example 10C.
Actual Situation: At bedtime daddy makes Toby some hot chocolate.

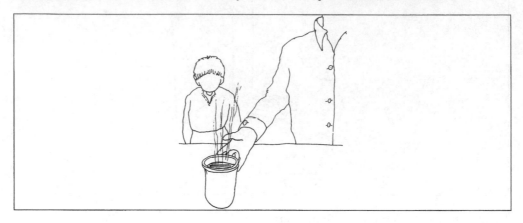

This is Toby. This picture tells us what Toby wants.
Desire: Toby wants some hot chocolate.
This picture tells us what Toby thinks.
Belief: Toby doesn't know about the hot chocolate. He thinks daddy has made him some orange juice.

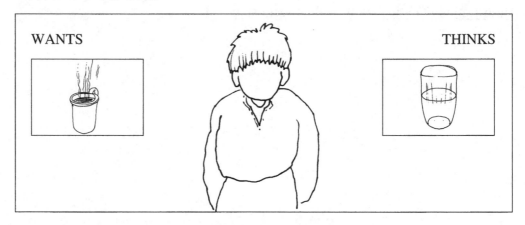

<u>Desire Question</u>: What does Toby want?
prompt — look, this picture tells us what Toby wants.
<u>Belief Question</u>: What does Toby think?
prompt — look, this picture tells us what Toby thinks.
<u>Emotion Question</u>: Toby wants some hot chocolate. Toby thinks daddy has made him some orange juice. How does Toby feel?
prompt — does he feel happy/sad?
<u>Justification Question</u>: Why does he feel happy/sad?

Outcome: Daddy gives Toby the hot chocolate.

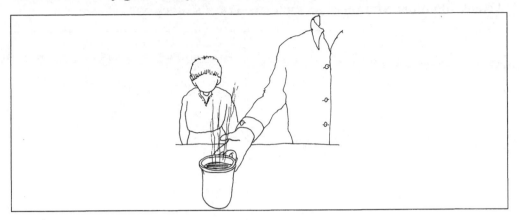

<u>Desire Question</u>: What does Toby want?
prompt — look, this picture tells us what Toby wants.

<u>Emotion Question</u>: How will Toby feel when daddy gives him the hot chocolate?
prompt — will he feel happy/sad?

<u>Justification Question</u>: Why will he feel happy/sad?

Example 11C.
Actual Situation: Mum has an apple for Tracy's lunch.

This is Tracy. This picture tells us what Tracy wants.
Desire: Tracy wants an apple.
This picture tells us what Tracy thinks.
Belief: Tracy doesn't know about the apple. She thinks mummy has a banana for her.

Desire Question: What does Tracy want?
prompt — look, this picture tells us what Tracy wants.
Belief Question: What does Tracy think?
prompt — look, this picture tells us what Tracy thinks.
Emotion Question: Tracy wants an apple. Tracy thinks mummy has a banana for her. How does Tracy feel?
prompt — does she feel happy/sad?
Justification Question: Why does she feel happy/sad?

Outcome: Mummy gives Tracy the apple for lunch.

<u>Desire Question</u>: What does Tracy want?
prompt — look, this picture tells us what Tracy wants.

<u>Emotion Question</u>: How will Tracy feel when mummy gives her the apple for lunch?
prompt — will she feel happy/sad?

<u>Justification Question</u>: Why will she feel happy/sad?

Example 12C.
Actual Situation: Jean's mum is taking her horse-riding.

This is Jean. This picture tells us what Jean wants.
Desire: Jean wants to go horse-riding.
This picture tells us what Jean thinks.
Belief: Jean doesn't know about the horse-riding. She thinks they are going dancing.

<u>Desire Question</u>: What does Jean want?
prompt — look, this picture tells us what Jean wants.
<u>Belief Question</u>: What does Jean think?
prompt — look, this picture tells us what Jean thinks.
<u>Emotion Question</u>: Jean wants to go horse riding. Jean thinks they are going dancing. How does Jean feel?
prompt — does she feel happy/sad?
<u>Justification Question</u>: Why does she feel happy/sad?

Outcome: Jean's mum takes her horse-riding.

<u>Desire Question</u>: What does Jean want?
prompt — look, this picture tells us what Jean wants.

<u>Emotion Question</u>: How will Jean feel when mummy takes her horse-riding?
prompt — will she feel happy/sad?

<u>Justification Question</u>: Why will she feel happy/sad?

Section D: False belief and unfulfilled desire
Example 1D.
Actual Situation: Betty's grandma buys Betty a teddy for her birthday.

This is Betty. This picture tells us what Betty wants.
Desire: Betty wants a doll.
This picture tells us what Betty thinks.
Belief: Betty doesn't know about the teddy. She thinks grandma has bought her a dolly.

Desire Question: What does Betty want?
prompt — look, this picture tells us what Betty wants.
Belief Question: What does Betty think?
prompt — look, this picture tells us what Betty thinks.
Emotion Question: Betty wants a doll. Betty thinks grandma has bought a doll. How does Betty feel?
prompt — does she feel happy/sad?
Justification Question: Why does she feel happy/sad?

Outcome: Betty's grandma buys her a teddy for her birthday.

<u>Desire Question</u>: What does Betty want?
prompt — look, this picture tells us what Betty wants.

<u>Emotion Question</u>: How will Betty feel when grandma gives her the doll?
prompt — will she feel happy/sad?

<u>Justification Question</u>: Why will she feel happy/sad?

Example 2D.
Actual Situation: Matthew's brother has a toy aeroplane for him.

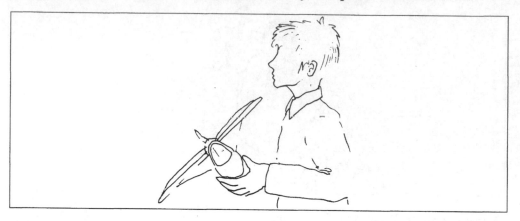

This is Matthew. This picture tells us what Matthew wants.
Desire: Matthew wants a toy train.
This picture tells us what Matthew thinks.
Belief: Matthew doesn't know about the aeroplane. He thinks his brother has bought a train for him.

<u>Desire Question</u>: What does Matthew want?
prompt — look, this picture tells us what Matthew wants.
<u>Belief Question</u>: What does Matthew think?
prompt — look, this picture tells us what Matthew thinks.
<u>Emotion Question</u>: Matthew wants a toy train. Matthew thinks his brother has a train. How does Matthew feel?
prompt — does he feel happy/sad?
<u>Justification Question</u>: Why does he feel happy/sad?

Outcome: Matthew's brother gives him the toy aeroplane.

<u>Desire Question</u>: What does Matthew want?
prompt — look, this picture tells us what Matthew wants.

<u>Emotion Question</u>: How will Matthew feel when his brother gives him the aeroplane?
prompt — will he feel happy/sad?

<u>Justification Question</u>: Why will he feel happy/sad?

Example 3D.
Actual Situation: At bedtime daddy makes Toby some hot chocolate.

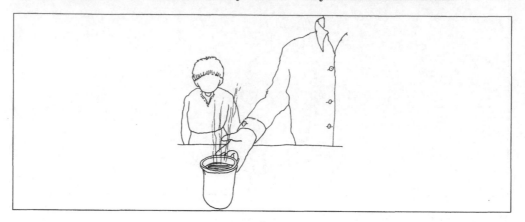

This is Toby. This picture tells us what Toby wants.
Desire: Toby wants some orange juice.
This picture tells us what Toby thinks.
Belief: Toby doesn't know about the chocolate. He thinks daddy has made him some orange juice.

<u>Desire Question</u>: What does Toby want?
prompt — look, this picture tells us what Toby wants.
<u>Belief Question</u>: What does Toby think?
prompt — look, this picture tells us what Toby thinks.
<u>Emotion Question</u>: Toby wants some orange juice. Toby thinks daddy has made him some orange juice. How does Toby feel?
prompt — does he feel happy/sad?
<u>Justification Question</u>: Why does he feel happy/sad?

Outcome: Daddy gives Toby the hot chocolate.

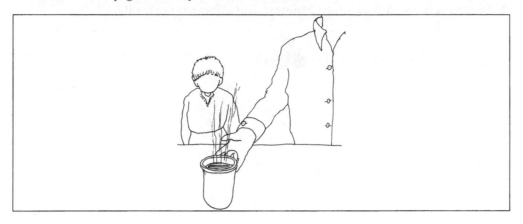

<u>Desire Question</u>: What does Toby want?
prompt — look, this picture tells us what Toby wants.

<u>Emotion Question</u>: How will Toby feel when daddy gives him the hot chocolate?
prompt — will he feel happy/sad?

<u>Justification Question</u>: Why will he feel happy/sad?

Example 4D.
Actual Situation: It's raining. Mummy buys Pat an umbrella.

This is Pat. This picture tells us what Pat wants.
Desire: Pat wants a rain hat.
This picture tells us what Pat thinks.
Belief: Pat doesn't know about the umbrella. She thinks mummy has bought her a rain hat.

<u>Desire Question</u>: What does Pat want?
prompt — look, this picture tells us what Pat wants.
<u>Belief Question</u>: What does Pat think?
prompt — look, this picture tells us what Pat thinks.
<u>Emotion Question</u>: Pat wants a rain hat. Pat thinks mummy has bought her a rain hat. How does Pat feel?
prompt — does she feel happy/sad?
<u>Justification Question</u>: Why does she feel happy/sad?

Outcome: Mummy gives Pat the umbrella.

<u>Desire Question</u>: What does Pat want?
prompt — look, this picture tells us what Pat wants.

<u>Emotion Question</u>: How will Pat feel when mummy gives her the umbrella?
prompt — will she feel happy/sad?

<u>Justification Question</u>: Why will she feel happy/sad?

Example 5D.
Actual Situation: Mummy has an apple for Tracy's lunch.

This is Tracy. This picture tells us what Tracy wants.
Desire: Tracy wants a banana.
This picture tells us what Tracy thinks.
Belief: Tracy doesn't know about the apple. She thinks mummy has a banana for her.

Desire Question: What does Tracy want?
prompt — look, this picture tells us what Tracy wants.
Belief Question: What does Tracy think?
prompt — look, this picture tells us what Tracy thinks.
Emotion Question: Tracy wants a banana. Tracy thinks mummy has a banana for her. How does Tracy feel?
prompt — does she feel happy/sad?
Justification Question: Why does she feel happy/sad?

Outcome: Mummy gives Tracy the apple for lunch.

<u>Desire Question</u>: What does Tracy want?
prompt — look, this picture tells us what Tracy wants.

<u>Emotion Question</u>: How will Tracy feel when mummy gives her the apple?
prompt — will she feel happy/sad?

<u>Justification Question</u>: Why will she feel happy/sad?

Example 6D.
Actual Situation: Brian's sister is taking him to the swimming pool.

This is Brian. This picture tells us what Brian wants.
Desire: Brian wants to go to the seaside.
This picture tells us what Brian thinks.
Belief: Brian doesn't know about the pool. He thinks they are going to the seaside.

Desire Question: What does Brian want?
prompt — look, this picture tells us what Brian wants.
Belief Question: What does Brian think?
prompt — look, this picture tells us what Brian thinks.
Emotion Question: Brian wants to go to the seaside. Brian thinks they are going to the seaside. How does Brian feel?
prompt — does he feel happy/sad?
Justification Question: Why does he feel happy/sad?

Outcome: Brian's sister takes him to the swimming pool.

Desire Question: What does Brian want?
prompt — look, this picture tells us what Brian wants.

Emotion Question: How will Brian feel when his sister takes him to the swimming pool?
prompt — will he feel happy/sad?

Justification Question: Why will he feel happy/sad?

Example 7D.
Actual Situation: Jean's mum is taking her horse riding.

This is Jean. This picture tells us what Jean wants.
Desire: Jean wants to go dancing.
This picture tells us what Jean thinks.
Belief: Jean doesn't know about the horse riding. She thinks they are going dancing.

Desire Question: What does Jean want?
prompt — look, this picture tells us what Jean wants.
Belief Question: What does Jean think?
prompt — look, this picture tells us what Jean thinks.
Emotion Question: Jean wants to go dancing. Jean thinks they are going dancing. How does Jean feel?
prompt — does she feel happy/sad?
Justification Question: Why does she feel happy/sad?

Outcome: Jean's mum takes her horse riding.

<u>Desire Question</u>: What does Jean want?
prompt — look, this picture tells us what Jean wants.

<u>Emotion Question</u>: How will Jean feel when her mum takes her horse riding?
prompt — will she feel happy/sad?

<u>Justification Question</u>: Why will she feel happy/sad?

Example 8D.
Actual Situation: The clowns will be at the circus.

This is Thomas. This picture tells us what Thomas wants.
Desire: Thomas wants to see the lions.
This picture tells us what Thomas thinks.
Belief: Thomas doesn't know about the clowns. He thinks the lions will be at the circus.

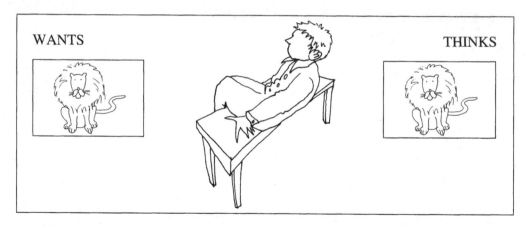

Desire Question: What does Thomas want?
prompt — look, this picture tells us what Thomas wants.
Belief Question: What does Thomas think?
prompt — look, this picture tells us what Thomas thinks.
Emotion Question: Thomas wants to see the lions. Thomas thinks the lions will be at the circus. How does Thomas feel?
prompt — does he feel happy/sad?
Justification Question: Why does he feel happy/sad?

Outcome: Thomas sees the clowns at the circus.

<u>Desire Question</u>: What does Thomas want?
prompt — look, this picture tells us what Thomas wants.

<u>Emotion Question</u>: How will Thomas feel when he sees the clowns at the circus?
prompt — will he feel happy/sad?

<u>Justification Question</u>: Why will he feel happy/sad?

Example 9D.
Actual Situation: The rope on Joanne's swing is broken.

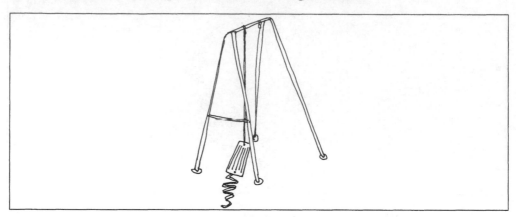

This is Joanne. This picture tells us what Joanne wants.
Desire: Joanne wants to play on her swing.
This picture tells us what Joanne thinks.
Belief: Joanne doesn't know the swing is broken. She thinks daddy has mended it.

Desire Question: What does Joanne want?
prompt — look, this picture tells us what Joanne wants.
Belief Question: What does Joanne think?
prompt — look, this picture tells us what Joanne thinks.
Emotion Question: Joanne wants to play on her swing. Joanne thinks daddy has mended it. How does Joanne feel?
prompt — does she feel happy/sad?
Justification Question: Why does she feel happy/sad?

Outcome: Joanne can't play on her swing. It's broken.

<u>Desire Question</u>: What does Joanne want?
prompt — look, this picture tells us what Joanne wants.

<u>Emotion Question</u>: How will Joanne feel when she can't play on her swing?
prompt — will she feel happy/sad?

<u>Justification Question</u>: Why will she feel happy/sad?

Example 10D.
Actual Situation: The handles have fallen off Marie's bike.

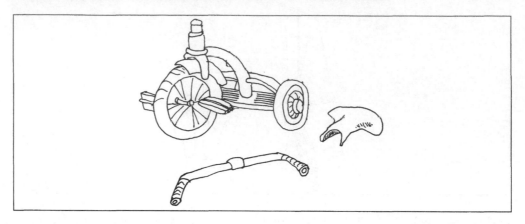

This is Marie. This picture tells us what Marie wants.
Desire: Marie wants to play on her bike.
This picture tells us what Marie thinks.
Belief: Marie doesn't know her bike is broken. She thinks daddy has mended it.

Desire Question: What does Marie want?
prompt — look, this picture tells us what Marie wants.
Belief Question: What does Marie think?
prompt — look, this picture tells us what Marie thinks.
Emotion Question: Marie wants to play on her bike. Marie thinks daddy has mended it. How does Marie feel?
prompt — does she feel happy/sad?
Justification Question: Why does she feel happy/sad?

Outcome: Marie can't play on her bike. It's broken.

<u>Desire Question</u>: What does Marie want?
prompt — look, this picture tells us what Marie wants.

<u>Emotion Question</u>: How will Marie feel when she can't play on her bike?
prompt — will she feel happy/sad?

<u>Justification Question</u>: Why will she feel happy/sad?

Example 11D.
Actual Situation: It's time for Adam's granddad to go home.

This is Adam. This picture tells us what Adam wants.
Desire: Adam wants his granddad to stay.
This picture tells us what Adam thinks.
Belief: Adam doesn't know his granddad is going. He thinks granddad is staying.

Desire Question: What does Adam want?
prompt — look, this picture tells us what Adam wants.
Belief Question: What does Adam think?
prompt — look, this picture tells us what Adam thinks.
Emotion Question: Adam wants his granddad to stay. Adam thinks granddad is staying. How does Adam feel?
prompt — does he feel happy/sad?
Justification Question: Why does he feel happy/sad?

Outcome: Adam's granddad says goodbye and goes home.

<u>Desire Question</u>: What does Adam want?
prompt — look, this picture tells us what Adam wants.

<u>Emotion Question</u>: How will Adam feel when his granddad goes home?
prompt — will he feel happy/sad?

<u>Justification Question</u>: Why will he feel happy/sad?

Example 12D.
Actual Situation: Kim's daddy has to go away on a trip.

This is Kim. This picture tells us what Kim wants.
Desire: Kim wants to go with her daddy.
This picture tells us what Kim thinks.
Belief: Kim doesn't know daddy is leaving her. She thinks she is going with him.

<u>Desire Question</u>: What does Kim want?
prompt — look, this picture tells us what Kim wants.
<u>Belief Question</u>: What does Kim think?
prompt — look, this picture tells us what Kim thinks.
<u>Emotion Question</u>: Kim wants to go with her daddy. Kim thinks she is going with him. How does Kim feel?
prompt — does she feel happy/sad?
<u>Justification Question</u>: Why does she feel happy/sad?

Outcome: Kim's daddy goes away on a trip.

<u>Desire Question</u>: What does Kim want?
prompt — look, this picture tells us what Kim wants.

<u>Emotion Question</u>: How will Kim feel when her daddy goes away?
prompt — will she feel happy/sad?

<u>Justification Question</u>: Why will she feel happy/sad?

Part III
Teaching about
informational states

In this section we describe teaching methods for the next class of mental states, the *informational states*. These include perception, knowledge and belief.

THE FIVE LEVELS OF INFORMATIONAL STATE UNDERSTANDING

Level 1. Simple visual perspective taking
This is the understanding that different people can see different things. At this level the child can judge what you (the teacher) can see or not see.

Level 2. Complex visual perspective taking
This involves understanding not only what people see but how it appears to them. This level requires the child to judge both what another person can see and HOW it appears to that person.

Level 3. Understanding the principle that "seeing leads to knowing"
This is the ability to understand that people only know things that they have experienced (directly or indirectly). In this teaching programme, we simplify this level by only assessing the link between SEEING and KNOWING, though of course there are also links between HEARING or FEELING and KNOWING.

Level 4. Predicting actions on the basis of a person's knowledge
This tests the child's understanding of *True Belief*. Here, children are required to predict a person's actions on the basis of where that person believes an object to be.

Level 5. Understanding false beliefs
This level assesses the child's ability to understand *False Belief*, the standard approach to theory of mind reasoning. Here children are required to predict a person's actions on the basis of where that person **falsely** believes an object to be.

LEVEL 1: SIMPLE VISUAL PERSPECTIVE TAKING

This is the understanding that different people can see different things. At this level the child can judge what you (the teacher) can see or not see.

Materials and assessment procedures

<u>A variety of different pictures</u> made up by the teacher (one picture on each side of the card), e.g.:
1. A pen/A key.
2. A dog/A tree.
3. A telephone/A flower.
4. A car/A snake, etc. (See Figure 3.1.)

Establishing a baseline

Hold up a large card, selected from the ones you have made up, between you and the child, with a different picture on each side. Then ask the child:

<u>Self-perception Question</u>: **"What can you see?"**
<u>Other-perception Question</u>: **"What can I see?"**

For the self-perception question the child simply has to label the object in front of him/her. For the other-perception question the correct answer, of course, must refer to the picture on the teacher's side of the card.

Note that it is very important to alternate or "counterbalance" the order of "What can you see?" and "What can I see"; otherwise many correct responses could just occur by chance. If the child fails to pass one or more trials from three in a row start teaching at this level.

Figure 3.1. Materials and procedures used in assessing and teaching simple visual perspective taking

Hold up the card between you and the child so that the child can see the picture on one side of the card and you can see the picture on the other side.

Side 1: Child's picture
<u>Self-perception Question</u>: What can you see?

Side 2: Teacher's picture

Teaching procedures

The teacher holds up an object and questions the child about what each of them can see, in turn.

Example:
Hold up a card (e.g. cake/teapot) between yourself and child

Self-perception Question: **"What can you see?"**
Other-perception Question: **"What can I see?"** (remember to vary the order of I/you)

Teaching:
Other-perception Question: For an incorrect response:
You can see the cake, can't you? The cake is on your side of the card.

Point to the picture facing the child.

But look! What is on my side of the card? What can I see?
Show the child the other side of the card.

That's right. I can see the teapot.

Face the card so the child can see the cake again.

I can't see the pen, only you can see the cake.

As at every level, if the response is correct the teacher reinforces this and strengthens the child's understanding by asking "What" they can both see in turn. If the response is incorrect, the correct answer is provided, as is the reason for this.

General teaching principle

Whether correct or incorrect the child is always provided with the general principle underlying that belief:

People do not always see the same thing, and what they see will depend on their position, etc.

LEVEL 2: COMPLEX VISUAL PERSPECTIVE TAKING

This involves understanding not only what people see but how it appears to them. This level requires the child to judge both what another person can see, and HOW it appears to that person.

Materials and assessment procedures

Set of pictures selected by the teacher and made up of items that are of interest to the child, e.g.:
1. Mickey Mouse.
2. A teapot.
3. An alarm clock.
4. An elephant, etc. (See Figure 3.2.)

Establishing a baseline

Place a large card with a picture on it between you and the child, flat on the table or floor, so that the object depicted appears one way up to you and the other way up to the child. For example, if the picture is of an elephant, to the child the elephant is the right way up but to you the elephant is upside down.

You then ask the child:

Other-perception Question:

"When I look at the picture, is [the elephant] right way up, or upside down?"

The presentation of the picture to the child should be counterbalanced so that on some trials the child sees the picture the correct way up and on other trials the picture is upside down. This is important, otherwise the child could score many "correct" responses simply by repeating the last few words of the question.

If the child fails to pass one or more trials from three in a row you should start teaching at this level.

Figure 3.2. Materials and procedures used in assessing and teaching complex visual perspective taking

Place the card between you and the child so that either you or the child can see the picture the right way up and either you or the child can see the picture upside down.

View 1: The child's perspective of the picture

<u>Self-perception Question</u>: When you look at the picture, is the elephant the right way up or is it upside down?

View 2: The teacher's perspective of the picture

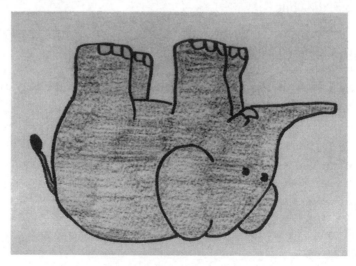

<u>Other-perception Question</u>: When I look at the picture, is the elephant the right way up or is it upside down?

Teaching procedures

The teacher questions the child about the position of an object that each of them sees from a different perspective.

Example: *Place the picture card (e.g. Mickey Mouse) on the table between child and adult, so that the object appears one way up to the child and the other way up to the adult. Then ask the child:*

Other-perception Question: **"When I look at the picture, is Mickey the right way up, or upside down?"** (vary the order of this choice)

Teaching
Other-perception Question: (For an incorrect response)
Look, when you look at Mickey, he is the right way up.
But when I look at Mickey he is upside down.
Watch what happens when I turn the card around.

Turn the card around so that to the child Mickey is upside down and to you he is the right way around.

Now, when I look at Mickey he is the right way around, but when you look at him he is upside down.

(Another teaching method that may be utilized is for the picture to remain in the same position and the child and experimenter to change seats in order to highlight the different perspectives.)

As at every level, if the response is correct the teacher reinforces this and strengthens the child's understanding by asking "Why?" "What happens?" etc. If the response is incorrect, the correct answer is provided, as is the reason for this.

General teaching principle

Whether correct or incorrect the child is always provided with the general principle underlying the belief:

People can see the same thing in different ways.

LEVEL 3: UNDERSTANDING
THE PRINCIPLE THAT "SEEING LEADS
TO KNOWING"

This tests the child's ability to understand that people only know things that they have experienced (directly or indirectly). As noted earlier in this teaching programme, we simplify this level by only assessing the link between SEEING and KNOWING (though of course there are also links between HEARING or FEELING and KNOWING).

Materials and assessment procedures

1. Various containers
2. A doll or puppet
3. Objects differing in size only e.g.:
     Big silver key/Small silver key.
     Big green crayon/Small green crayon.
     Big yellow die/Small yellow die.
     Big red ball/Small red ball.
4. Objects differing in colour only e.g.:
     One yellow pencil/One green pencil.
     One pink ball/One blue ball.
     One green button/One white button.
     One red ribbon/One blue ribbon.

As far as possible the items used should be objects that are of interest to the child or are part of everyday activites. (See Figure 3.3.)

Figure 3.3. Materials and procedures used in assessing and teaching "seeing leads to knowing"

Here are examples of some of the materials used in the "seeing leads to knowing" task.

Examples of boxes that can be used to hide objects in.

Examples of pairs of objects to hide: Objects that differ only in colour.

Examples of pairs of objects to hide: Objects that differ only in size.

Establishing a baseline

Two examples of how to assess Level 3, one self-judgement (Section A) and one other-judgement (Section B) are given here. The assessment should include an example from each section plus one additional example.

In these tasks you should simply put one item, from each pair chosen, into a box, whilst asking the child *either* to watch, or to keep his or her eyes closed.

Section A. Self-judgement

<u>Materials</u>: One box/One big green crayon/One small green crayon.

Let's play a hiding game with this box.
Look at these crayons. This crayon is big and this crayon is little.

I am going to hide one of the crayons in the box. Can you close your eyes so you can't see which one I put in there?

Hide the big crayon in the box.

<u>Knowledge Question</u>: **Do you know which crayon is in the box?**
[No]

<u>Justification Question</u>: **"Why don't you know which crayon is in the box?**
[Because I didn't see, etc]

Section B. Other-judgement

<u>Materials</u>: One box/One doll/One yellow ball/One blue ball.

Now, let's play another hiding game with the tunnel.
Claire can play too. Here is Claire.

(Present the doll—Claire)

Let's show Claire the balls.
Look Claire, this ball is blue and this ball is yellow.
Now, we'll hide one of the balls in the box.
Let's put Claire down here so she can't see which ball we put into the box.

Which ball should we put into the box? Can you choose one.

The child should be encouraged to choose one of the balls and hide it in the box. If he/she doesn't do this then the teacher should hide the yellow ball in the box.

Claire is coming back now.
Now, we'll let Claire look at the ball in the box.

Move Claire so she can see in the box.

<u>Knowledge Question</u>: **Does Claire know which ball is in the box?**
[Yes]

<u>Justification Question</u>: **How does Claire know it is the yellow/blue ball?**
[She looked]

If the child fails on one of the three Level 3 tasks you have selected, then begin teaching at this level.

Teaching procedures

The teacher hides an object, which the child cannot see, and then questions him/her about their knowledge of this.

There are two versions of this task: self-judgement and other-judgement.

<u>Example</u>: **Self-judgement**

Let's play a hiding game with this box.
Look at these crayons. This crayon is big and this crayon is little.
I am going to hide one of these crayons in the box.
Can you close your eyes so you can't see which one I put in there?

Hide one of the crayons in the box and ask the child to uncover his or her eyes.

<u>Knowledge Question</u>: **Do you know which crayon is in the box?**

<u>Justification Question</u>: **How do you know/Why don't you know which crayon is in there?**

<u>Teaching</u>

<u>Knowledge Question</u>: For an incorrect response.

You didn't see which crayon I put in the box, so you don't know that the big crayon is in there. If you don't see, then you don't know!

As at every level, if the response is correct the teacher reinforces this and strengthens the child's understanding by asking "Why"; 'How" they know what they do. If the response is incorrect, the correct answer is provided, along with a reason for this answer.

General teaching principle

Whether correct or incorrect, the child is always provided with the general principle underlying the belief.

People only know about things they have seen. If they can't see something, then they don't know about it.

LEVEL 4: PREDICTING ACTIONS ON THE BASIS OF A PERSON'S KNOWLEDGE

This tests the child's understanding that people can hold *true beliefs*. Here, children are required to make action predictions on the basis of where another person believes an object to be.

Materials and assessment procedures

A desk-top house:
Rooms/locations to put objects in:

Various items of toy furniture:

Objects (to be placed in different locations).
e.g.
1. Two red balls
2. Two umbrellas.
3. Two crayons.
4. Two books, etc.

Again, choose items that the child is interested in as far as possible. (See Figure 3.4.)

Figure 3.4. Materials and procedures used in assessing and teaching "true belief" understanding

Here is an example of a true belief story using Bill, two toy buses and the desk-top house.

Let's play a game with this house and Bill.
Look, there is a bus on the table and there is a bus on the shelf.

Here is Bill.
This morning Bill saw the bus on the table but he didn't see the bus on the shelf.

Belief Question: Where does Bill think the bus is?
Justification Question: Why does he think it is on the shelf?
Action Question: Where will Bill go to get the bus?
Justification Question: Why will he go to the table/shelf?

Establishing a baseline

One example of how to assess true belief is given below. Two additional examples should be selected using the sorts of materials suggested above.

<u>Materials</u>: Desk-top house with two rooms/doll or puppet (Bill)/two locations, bed (in bedroom) and table (in kitchen).

Let's play a game with this house and Bill.
Look, there is a ball on the bed and there is a ball on the table.

Indicate both locations to the child.

Here is Bill

Bill faces the teacher and the child and away from the house.

This morning Bill saw the ball on the bed. Bill didn't see the ball on the table.

Point appropriately.

<u>Belief Question</u>: **Where does Bill think the ball is?** [On the bed]

<u>Justification Question</u>: **Why does he think it is on the bed?**

If the child fails one out of the three stories you have given in the assessment, then begin the teaching here.

Teaching procedures

The teacher involves the child in a game incorporating a toy person and a selection of other objects and asks about the toy's character knowledge of and response to those objects.

Example: **Let's play a game with this house and Bill.**
Look, there is a ball on the bed and there is a ball on the table

Here is Bill, this morning Bill saw the ball on the bed. Bill didn't see the ball on the table.

Point appropriately.

Action Question: **Where will Bill go to get the ball?**

Justification Question: **Why does he think it is on the bed?**

Check Question: **Where did Bill see the ball?**

Teaching

Teaching Question: For an incorrect response.

Remember, Bill saw the ball on the bed, so Bill will look for the ball on the bed.

Bill didn't see the ball on the table so he won't look there.

As at every level, if the response is correct the teacher reinforces this and strengthens the child's understanding by tasking "Where?" the character will look; "Why?" he will do so etc. If the response is incorrect, the correct answer is provided, as are the reasons for the character acting in this way.

General teaching principle

Whether correct or incorrect the child is always provided with the general principle underlying the belief:

People think things are where they saw them. If they didn't see something then they won't know they are there.

LEVEL 5: UNDERSTANDING FALSE BELIEFS

This level assesses the child's ability to understand that people can hold *false beliefs*, the standard approach to theory of mind reasoning. We suggest using two common variants of this task:

A. The *unexpected transfer* task
B. The *unexpected contents* task.

In this section we describe various toys that can be used in the teaching of false beliefs, and in Part IV we also describe different computer programmes that can be used in teaching. The initial assessment should include at least one of the variants of each task. Two examples of how to assess false belief are given below. An additional example should be selected using materials such as those suggested below.

Materials and assessment procedures

A. The *unexpected transfer* task

1. **A desk-top house** — with choice of locations.
        various items of toy furniture
2. **Doll or puppet figures**
3. **Containers/Objects:**
        Two purses (black/red).
        Two plastic beakers (blue/yellow).
        Two cardboard boxes (yellow/red).
        Two cupboards.
        Penny.
        Ball.
        Umbrella.
        Watering can.
        Or any objects that are of particular interest to the child. (See Figure 3.5.)

Figure 3.5. Materials and procedures used in assessing and teaching "false belief" understanding (unexpected transfer tasks)

Here is an example of a false belief unexpected transfer story using two characters Kate and Bill, one toy car and the desk-top house.

Let's play a game with this house and Kate and Bill.
Look, Kate puts her toy car on the bed.

Kate is going out to play. Bill has gone out now and she can't see what Bill is doing.

Bill plays a trick on Kate. He puts the toy car into the cupboard.

Here comes Kate back from the playground.

Belief Question: Where does Kate think the toy car is? [in the cupboard].
Justification Question: Why does she think it is on the bed/in the cupboard?

Action Question: Where will Kate go to get the toy car?
Justification Question: Why will she go to the bed/cupboard?

B. The *unexpected contents* task

Box:
Crayon box
Smarties packet (chocolate buttons)
Match box
Play-doh container

Unexpected contents:
Toy car
Pencil
Plastic buttons
Sand, etc.

Figure 3.6. Materials and procedures used in assessing and teaching "false belief" understanding (unexpected contents tasks)

Here is an example of a false belief unexpected contents task using a Smarties packet, a pencil and a doll.

Here is a sweet packet.

Initial Belief Question: What do you think is inside this packet?

Let's have a look and see what is in here. Can you open the packet?

Look there is a pencil in there. Let's close the packet again.
False Belief Question: Before we opened the packet what did you think was in here?
Reality Question: And what is really in here?

Look here comes Rosie.

<u>Other Belief Question</u>: Rosie comes in and looks at the sweet packet, what will she think is inside?

Establishing a baseline

(a) Unexpected transfer

<u>Materials</u>: Doll, a black purse and a red purse, and a penny

---

Let's play a game with Claire.

Look Claire has a penny.

Here are two purses, a black purse and a red purse.
Claire puts her penny into the black purse.

Claire is going out to play now.

Claire walks out of the room.

Claire has gone out. She can't see what we are doing.

Shall we play a trick on Claire? We'll take the penny out of the black purse and put it in the green purse.

<u>Belief Question</u>: **Here comes Claire back from the playground. Where does Claire think the penny is?**
[In the black purse]

<u>Justification Question</u>: **Why does Claire think it is in the [black] purse?**

(b) Unexpected contents

<u>Materials</u>: Sweet packet/Buttons.

Look, here is a sweet packet.

<u>Initial Belief Question</u>: **What do you think is inside this packet?**
[Sweets]

**Let's have a look and see what is in here. Can you open the packet?
Look there are buttons in there!
Let's close the packet again.**

<u>False Belief Question</u>: **Before we opened the box what did you think
was in there?**
[Sweets]

<u>Reality Question</u>: **And what is in here really?**
[Buttons]

<u>Other Belief Question</u>: **If Suzie comes in and looks at this sweet
packet, what will she think is inside?**
[Sweets]

If the child fails one of the three tasks in Level 5 that you have chosen for the
assessment then begin the teaching here.

Teaching procedures

The teacher plays "tricks" on toy characters by removing their possessions etc. and then questions the child about the characters' beliefs about what has happened.

Example 1: Unexpected transfer.
Let's play a game with Claire. Look Claire has a penny.

Here are two purses, a black purse and a red purse.

Claire puts her penny into the black purse.
Claire is going out to play now.

Claire walks out of the room.

Claire has gone out. She can't see what we are doing.

Shall we play a trick on Claire? We'll take the penny out of the black purse and put it in the red purse!

Here comes Claire, back from the playground.

Belief Question: **Where does Claire think the penny is?**

Justification Question: **Why does Claire think it is in the [black] purse?**

Check Question: **Where did Claire put the penny?**

Teaching

Belief Question: For an incorrect response.

Remember, Claire didn't see us hide the penny in the red purse, so Claire doesn't know there is a penny in the red purse. She won't think it is in there. Claire will think the penny is in the black purse, because she put the penny in the black purse.

Example 2: Unexpected contents.
Look, here is a sweet packet.

Initial Belief Question: **What do you think is inside this packet?**
[Sweets]

Let's have a look and see what is in here. Can you open the packet?
Look there are buttons in there! Isn't that funny!
Let's close the packet again.

False Belief Question: **Before we opened the box what did you think**
was in there?
[Sweets]

Reality Question: **And what is in here really?**
[Buttons]

Other Belief Question: **If Suzie comes in and looks at this sweet**
packet, what will she think is inside?
[Sweets]

Teaching

Belief Question: For an incorrect response.

Remember, Suzie doesn't know this sweet packet has got buttons
in. She thinks there are sweets in it because it looks like a sweet
packet, doesn't it? Only we know that there are really buttons in
there.

As at every level, if the response is correct the teacher reinforces this and strengthens the child's understanding by asking "What?" the character will think and "Why?" etc. If the response is incorrect, the correct answer is provided, as are the reasons for the character thinking this way.

General teaching principle

Whether correct or incorrect the child is always provided with the general principle underlying the belief:

> **If people don't know that things have changed then they will think things are just the same.**

Part IV
Developing pretend play

In this section we turn to the final class of mental state terms for which we have developed a teaching programme: *pretence*. Once again, teaching is broken down into 5 levels.

THE FIVE LEVELS OF
PRETEND PLAY

Level 1. Sensorimotor play
This is when the child simply manipulates toys. It includes banging, waving or sucking objects. It also includes ritualistic or stereotyped behaviours, such as lining up toys or sorting them by size or colour.

Level 2. Emerging functional play
This occurs when the child uses toys in a socially conventional way, but with no pretence (e.g.: putting a cup on a saucer; pushing a car along). Children are scored as reaching this level if they show one or two examples of such play during a 10-minute recorded session.

Level 3. Established functional play
Children are scored as reaching this level if they demonstrate at least three or more examples of functional play during a 10-minute recorded sessions with sets of toys.

Level 4(a). Emerging pretend play
Pretend play includes:

(i) **Object substitution:** where one object is made to stand in for another object. For example, a child may pretend that a wooden block is a car.
(ii) **Attribution of pretend properties:** This involves attributing false properties to an object in play. For example, when a child cleans his/her doll's face as if it were dirty.

(iii) **Use of imaginary objects/scenarios:** A child is seen to use imaginary objects in play when he/she behaves as if absent objects were present. This would include, for example, drinking tea from an empty cup or making a car have an imaginary collision.

This level is scored if the child *spontaneously* produces one or two examples of any of the above during a 10-minute recorded session with sets of toys.

Level 4(b). The pretend–real distinction
Here the teacher performs a pretend action and then asks the child if she is REALLY doing it, or just PRETENDING. If the child answers correctly this is scored. Examples and materials for this are given below.

Level 5. Established pretend play
This level is scored if the child *spontaneously* produces at least three or more or two examples of any of the types of play listed in Level 4(a) above, during a 10-minute recorded session.

ASSESSING AND TEACHING PRETEND PLAY

Below we suggest several play schemes and possible materials. However, as much imagination and flexibility as possible should be used in introducing additional play themes, particularly those that fit in with the individual child's interests. The child's mental age also needs to be taken into consideration when choosing appropriate activities. In working with children with autism it is important that chronological age alone should not be used to determine the choice of toys, but that materials should be as relevant as possible to the child's developmental level.

Because assessment is difficult during an ongoing play session it is recommended that sessions are video-taped at the time, if possible, and rated later. Assessment sessions should last approximately 10 minutes.

Suggested materials and play themes

Dinner time
Toy cooking/eating utensils.

Shopping
Dolls/shopping equipment/toy basket, etc.

In the park
Play people,
push-chair/baby/swing/roundabout, etc.

Driving
Numerous play/people/cars.
Road signs/lights/garages, etc.

Dressing up
Pictures:
Policeman/witch/fireman
Clothes etc.
Police/firemen/witch hats.
Steering wheel, cloaks, magic wand, etc.

In addition to using these themes and materials, it is also suggested that the teacher make good use of any "junk material", which lends itself to object substitution. Some examples are given below:

Junk material
Set of wooden bricks.
Painted boxes.
Coloured plasticine.
Squares of coloured material.
Lengths of coloured ribbon.
Coloured paper shapes.
Fluorescent coloured circles.
Squares of tinfoil.
Pairs of shoelaces.
Balls of cotton wool.
Plastic straws.
Cocktail stirrers.
Pieces of plain card.

Establishing a baseline

Assessing spontaneous play — Levels 1, 2, 3, 4(a) and 5

Encourage the child to play, using one of the play themes listed above and let this continue for 10 minutes, without help (less if the child is completely "off-task"). The level of play can then be established following the definitions in Section 5.1.

The level at which teaching begins will be the level above that spontaneously reached by the child.

Assessing the pretend–real distinction – Level 4(b)

For assessing the pretend–real distinction we suggest three examples, one involving object substitution and the others pretend actions. However, the teacher should feel free to elaborate on these basic plots, so as to generate at least three examples for the assessment.

Example 1. Object substitution.
Materials: Piece of string.

Let's play some pretend games.
Look at this! It's a piece of string. We can pretend that it's something else.
Let's pretend it's [a snake].

Act as if the string were a snake making appropriate noises and actions. The teacher might say for example:
"Look at the snake sliding through the grass, listen to the noise it is making, ssssss...".

I'm pretending this is a snake, do you want to pretend it's a snake?

Then ask the test questions:
Reality Question: Is this really a snake?

Pretend Question: **Am I pretending this is a snake, or am I pretending this is string?**

Example 2. Pretend action: brushing one's teeth.

> **Now let's play another pretend game.**
> **Watch me. I'm going to pretend to do something.**
> **I'm going to pretend to brush my teeth.**
>
> *Act as if you are brushing your teeth with an imaginary toothbrush.*
>
> **I'm pretending to brush my teeth. Can you pretend to brush your teeth too?**
>
> *Continue to pretend brushing and then ask the test question:*
>
> Reality Question: **Is this really a toothbrush?**
>
> Pretend Question: **Am I pretending, or am I really brushing my teeth?**

Example 3. Pretend scenario: washing a doll's face.

Material: Toy doll

> **Here's another game now.** (Take toy doll)
> **Watch me pretend to wash dolly's face.**
> **I'm going to pretend that she's really dirty.**
>
> *Act as if you are washing the doll's face with an imaginary flannel.*
>
> **I'm pretending her face is dirty and needs a good wash. Can you pretend she needs a wash too?**
>
> *Continue to pretend washing and then ask the test question:*
>
> Reality Question: **Is dolly's face really dirty?**
>
> Pretend Question: **Am I pretending her face is dirty or is it really dirty?**

Teaching the pretend–real distinction should begin if the child fails either the reality or pretend questions on any of the three tasks presented.

Teaching procedures

Increasing the level of pretend play

Having established the child's basal level, the aim is to "push" the child up to the next level. For example, if the child's basal level is functional play (Level 2), encourage more examples of this type of play to help the child to succeed at Level 3.

Boxes 4.1–4.3 indicate how patterns of spontaneous, but not particularly imaginative play, can be developed into more symbolic and shared play activities.

An example from part of an "In the Park" play session.
Billy[1] is a very able young boy aged nine and a half years. His verbal mental age is nine years.

Box 4.1
A transcribed example of spontaneous play

Billy got the swing from the box and pushes it to and fro. Billy then spun the roundabout to make it go round and round. Billy took some plastic buttons from the "junk" box and threw them up into the air and caught them. Billy picked up one of the play dolls and tried to put a hat on it. Billy then picked up a straw and blew through it. Billy took some plastic rings from the "junk" box, threw them up and caught them. He then picked up a cardboard circle and fanned himself with it before throwing it up into the air and catching it. Billy spun the roundabout again, he then picked the roundabout up and spun it while holding it. Billy threw the plastic rings up again and caught them, he then rolled one of them across the table catching it and spinning it on his finger. Billy threw some plastic buttons up again and caught them, he then looked through the junk box in search of more buttons. Unable to find buttons Billy picked out some cardboard and then replaced it in the box. Billy went back to the toys, putting the baby doll into the pram. He picked up a plastic circle again and spun it on his finger.

---

1. "Billy" is a fictitious name

Boxes 4.2 and 4.3 describe two examples from the play teaching session that followed the above spontaneous play. These are presented as the dialogue which takes place between the teacher and Bill. The first example comes from the beginning of the play session where play is focused very much on the *functional* aspects of the objects. The second example is taken from the middle of the play session where the teacher introduces more symbolic play with the use of the junk materials available. Explanatory notes have been added to the transcript in order to make clear what is actually happening during the session.

Box 4.2. Developing spontaneous play: example 1

Transcript

T . . . Can you do one of them for me because I can't do them all.

B What do we do after this?

T You do that one and I'll do these ones, look there are lots to put on here.

B Where? Here?

T That's it.

B There.

T Put his arms up and help him to hold on.

B There.

T That's it, can you help me put them on? Help me put this little boy on.

B May I send it round fast? Yes?

T That's it, help me put it on, then we can spin it around fast yes.

B I need some help.

T Do you?

B I can't, I need some help.

T Just put his arms out like this, make him sit down and then you can put him on. Put his hands on there, that's it. Put the other hand on.

B Oh!

T Like that. There, very good. Can you put her on as well and I'll put this little girl on.

B There. Is this just pretend?

Explanatory Notes

The teacher encourages Billy to put the play people onto the roundabout i.e. to use the toys in a functional way. Billy initially walks around the room and then he sits down on the floor next to the teacher and helps her to put the children onto the roundabout.

Once this task has been done Billy sits back, throws a plastic button up into the air and catches it several times.

The teacher brings Billy back into the play situation by asking him to do a specific task. Billy goes back to the roundabout and he asks for help with the task — which the teacher gives.

Billy continues with the task.

T   That's right, we'll just pretend, would you like to put her on there? And put her hands on.

B   I can't.

Billy sits back and puts his head in his hands. Billy refuses to try again and watches while the teacher does it.

T   Whoops, try again.

B   No.

The teacher then asks an easier task of Billy in order to keep him in the play situation and Billy cooperates this time.

T   That one is done. Can you press this one down? That's it, well done. Now we've got five children on the roundabout.

B   What can I do?

T   Do you think you can turn them around?

B   I did that, see?

Billy spins the children on the roundabout.

T   Yes, they're going "Weeee! We're having lots of fun!"

B   Should I spin them around lots?

The teacher introduces some pretend play to the situation — making the children speak.

T   They are going backwards! Better push them forwards.

B   That way?

T   That's it. Ooooo crash!

B   Oh, come on.

Billy spins the roundabout both ways and one of the play people falls off. Billy hands this person to the teacher to put back on the roundabout.

T   Better help. Is he hurt? Oh dear, that's it, put him back on again. Better hold on with two hands this time.

B   Coming off to carry me home.

Billy puts the person back onto the roundabout with the teacher's help.

T   Spin them around. This boy is going to push the baby.

B   Push the baby? Look!

Billy starts to lose interest again — he sings to himself and starts to spin the roundabout again.

T   Push the baby and the baby's going to sleep. Is the baby asleep yet?

Billy moves away from the play — he picks up a plastic button and throws it up into the air and catches it several times

. . .

Box 4.3. Developing spontaneous play: example 2

Transcript

T . . . What shall we do next then? What would you like to do? Shall we make a pond?

B Shall we do that?

T Shall we? What could we use as a pond?

B Shall we? Can you help me?

T I'll help you.

B Look!

T Shall we use that as a pond?

B Don't!

T Shall we use that as a pond?

B I like blowing wind.

T Oh do you? It is a windy day today? What could we use as a pond?

B I like blowing things. I like using different things for blowing wind.

T Shall we use this as a pond? Shall we finish playing this and then we'll go home? Shall we use this as a pond?

B Look!

T Oooo! Put that down! What else do we need in a pond? Can you find some ducks? What could we use as a duck?

B I'll find something.

T What's this Billy? "Quack, quack, quack, quack."

B Can I stick this together?

T Are you going to use that to make another duck? Shall we make two ducks? Would you like to?

Explanatory Notes

The teacher has used all the play park equipment in a functional capacity. The teacher moves away from the functional properties of the toys and, with the use of the junk box, introduces more pretence.

Billy goes to the junk box and begins to rummage through it.

He finds a rectangle-shaped card and wafts it in the air towards the teacher's face. The teacher immediately brings this card into the play context — by asking if it is a windy day.

Billy starts to waft the card at his own face.

The teacher directs Billy's attention away from the card/home and suggests that they use a green circle as a pond.

Billy takes the circle and puts it on the floor. He then picks up a straw and puts it in his mouth — asking the teacher to look at him.

The teacher brings his attention back to the task and Billy responds by looking for a "duck" in the junk box. Billy finds the rectangle again and begins to waft it. The teacher makes a duck from some plasticine. Billy finds some more plasticine.

The teacher suggests that he uses this plasticine to make another duck.

The teacher helps Billy to find more plasticine.

B I can't see any more.

T Here's a little bit.

B Shall we use that here?

T Shall we put him in the pond? *The teacher suggests that they put the duck in the pond.*

B In here? *Billy does and he then picks up the whole pond and uses it to throw the duck into the air and catch it.*

T That's very good. Whoops careful, you had better put the pond down. Put the pond down. *When the teacher asks him to put the pond down Billy moves away from the play situation.*

B No.

T Billy, shall we take the children to feed the ducks? *The teacher makes another new suggestion to bring him back —feeding the ducks.*

B Shall we? *Billy comes and sits back down.*

T Shall I find some duck food? *Billy rummages through the box.*

B Can you help me?

T What could we use as duck food?

B Look! *Billy picks up a skipping rope and shows it to the teacher.*

T What's that?

B A skipping rope.

T A skipping rope, shall we pretend it is something else in the park? *The teacher again uses what Billy has found and incorporates it into the play theme.*

B No.

T Shall we pretend it's a bush? Let's put the bush near the pond. Shall we find another bush? We can pretend this is a bush . . .? *The teacher puts the skipping rope in a small pile next to the pond and continues with the same theme. Billy continues to look through the box. He finds a button and plays with it.*

Level 4(b) Teaching the pretend–real distinction

Example 1. Object substitution.
<u>Materials</u>: Piece of string.

<u>If the child cannot answer the Reality Question:</u>

Make it clear that you're going to stop pretending.

OK we're going to stop playing now. Let's look at it carefully. Look, this is REALLY a piece of string, just like you tie your shoes with. It's not a snake is it! Of course it's not, we were just playing! What is it really . . . it's just a . . .

(Prompt if necessary until child provides correct response)

<u>If the child cannot answer the Pretend Question:</u>

Pretend the string is a snake again.

Look, this is a piece of string. *Point to the string.*
But I am PRETENDING this is a snake. *Act up as much as needed.*

Look, it's wriggling up to you . . . oh, I hope it's not going to bite me . . . Ow! It did, the naughty snake.

Are we pretending it's a snake, or are we pretending it's a piece of string? . . .

We're pretending it's a . . .
(Prompt if necessary until child provides correct response)

Example 2. Pretend action: brushing one's teeth.

<u>If the child cannot answer the Reality Question:</u>

Make it clear that you're going to stop pretending.

OK we're going to stop playing now. Let's look carefully — it's not really a toothbrush is it . . . Look, there's nothing there! What are we doing . . . we're just . . .

(Prompt if necessary until child provides correct response)

<u>If the child cannot answer the Pretend Question:</u>

Demonstrate the pretend action again.

Look, I am pretending to brush my teeth. I've got lots of toothpaste and I'm brushing really hard. I'm going to get my teeth really clean. Are you going to do yours too?

Are we pretending to brush our teeth or are we really brushing them? . . .

We're . . .

(Prompt if necessary until child provides correct response)

As at every level, if the response is correct the teacher reinforces this and strengthens the child's understanding by asking "What" people are pretending/doing etc. If the response is incorrect, the correct answer is provided.

General teaching principles

The general principles here are:

We can pretend something is something else.

Things stay as they really are even when people pretend they are something else.

or

People can pretend there is something there when really there is nothing there.

Part V
Future directions

In this Guide we have only included those methods that we have actually tried and tested in a treatment/educational context. However, we wish to make it clear that these methods certainly do not exhaust all of the possible ways in which mind-reading might be facilitated in children with autism. In this closing section we outline some possible directions for future work in this area.

USING A PERSON'S DIRECTION OF GAZE TO INFER WHAT A PERSON WANTS OR IS INTERESTED IN, OR WHAT THEY MIGHT BE INTENDING TO DO NEXT

Recent experimental studies[1] have found that young children with autism are relatively unaware of the significance of direction of a person's gaze as an outward indicator of what that person may want, intend, or find of interest. For example, given a display like that in Figure 5.1, and when asked "Which sweet does Charlie **want?**", children with autism frequently fail to use Charlie's eyes as a cue to Charlie's desire. Instead, they chose their own favourite. In contrast, young non-autistic children use direction of gaze as a "natural pointer" to infer a person's desires, goals, or interest. One idea, then, is that such tasks could be used in teaching children with autism to mindread.

USING PHOTOGRAPHS TO REPRESENT THOUGHTS AND BELIEFS

Another recent study we have completed[2] has established that if one teaches children with autism that "the mind is like a camera", this can lead to them passing

Figure 5.1. Which sweet does Charlie want? Reprinted from Baron-Cohen et al. (1995) with permission.

false belief tests. Note though that at present there is no evidence that this new ability generalizes very far, but we mention it here simply because extended use of this metaphor may turn out to be useful.

The method simply involves telling the child that every time a person looks at anything, their eye takes a picture of whatever is in front of them at the time. Teachers can make this idea even more concrete by suggesting that when a person's eye **blinks**, this is the **click** of a camera. Having taught the child that people thus have pictures just like photos in their heads which children with autism seem to grasp very easily, because they have seen cameras[3,4] the next step is to teach the child that when a person wants to find something, they will go to where the object was **in the photo** in their head. If when they were not present the object was moved, then they have a photo in their head which does not match reality, but the key is to teach the child that nevertheless it is the **outdated** or inaccurate photo that will indicate where the person will look for the object. This method looks promising, from our initial study.

Note that this method can also be made very concrete. For example, in our study, we first familiarized children with a camera (we used a Polaroid camera, since it gives an instant printout — instant gratification!). We then used a manikin's head with a slot cut into it, into which the child could post the Polaroid photograph of the scene the manikin was "looking" at. The whole method was thus lots of fun for the child, as well as being tailored to their educational needs.

USING "CARTOON THOUGHT-BUBBLES" TO REPRESENT BELIEFS

Our ongoing work is using an even simpler method, based on the photos-in-the-head approach, described in the previous section. This new method substitutes cartoon thought-bubbles for photographs. It is a simpler method because it can all be done using drawings—pen and paper, or a blackboard.

You can probably imagine how this works. The first step is to teach the child the conventions of cartoon thought-bubbles, and that what people have in their thought-bubbles depends on what they were **looking** at, at the time. The rest of the method is then identical to the photo method (above), but using the thought-bubble instead of the photo, as the key metaphor.

Ethical issues

We are aware of the potential ethical issues that arise in telling children with autism that people have photos or thought-bubbles in their heads. Since it is not literally true (as far as we know!), it is potentially misleading. Telling the child it is just a metaphor is probably **not** useful, but we have used a form of wording to get around this: "People have things that are **just like** photos (or bubbles) in their heads". Some teachers may not be too worried about this point, and may even consider this detail is unnecessary, especially as the **value** of telling children with autism that people have photos in their heads may outweigh the ethical concern that this is misleading. We simply raise this issue for consideration.

JOINT ATTENTION AND EMPATHY

Finally, other teachers might consider that the methods described in this Guide are rather artificial and didactic, and that real mindreading will only be fostered by focusing on its developmental precursors: joint attention[5,6] and/or empathy[7,8]. Such an alternative, more interpersonal approach may turn out to be valuable, and we would certainly encourage teachers to work in these areas, especially with those children who are less verbal, and for whom the methods in this Guide may be less accessible. In the end, we suspect that a combination of approaches may turn out to be of most benefit to children with autism. We look forward to hearing from you about what does and does not work, and to what extent. Trying is everything.

REFERENCES TO PART V

1. Baron-Cohen, S., Campbell, R., Karmiloff-Smith, A., Grant, J. and Walker, J. (1995). Are children with autism blind to the mentalistic significance of the eyes? *British Journal of Developmental Psychology.*
2. Swettenham, J.S., Gomez, J.-C., Baron-Cohen, S. and Walsh, S. (1996). What's inside a person's head? Conceiving of the mind as a camera helps children with autism develop an alternative theory of mind. *Cognitive Neuropsychiatry.*
3. Leslie, A.M. and Thaiss, L. (1992). Domain specificity in conceptual development: evidence from autism. *Cognition*, **43**, 225–251.
4. Leekham, S. and Perner, J. (1991). Does the autistic child have a metarepresentational deficit? *Cognition*, **40**, 203–218.
5. Baron-Cohen, S. (1989). Perceptual role-taking and protodeclarative pointing in autism. *British Journal of Developmental Psychology*, **7**, 113–127.
6. Baron-Cohen, S. (1994). How to build a baby that can read minds: Cognitive mechanisms in mindreading. *Cahiers de Psychologie Cognitive/Current Psychology of Cognition*, **13**(5), 513–552.
7. Yirmiya, N., Sigman, M., Kasari, C., and Mundy, P. (1992). Empathy and cognition in high functioning children with autism. *Child Development*, **63**, 150–160.
8. Hobson, R.P. (1993). Understanding persons: the role of affect. In S. Baron-Cohen, H. Tager-Flusberg and D.J. Cohen (eds). *Understanding Other Minds.* Oxford: Oxford University Press.

Appendix
Examples of record forms

Recording forms should be completed for each teaching/assessment session in order to monitor progress as systematically as possible. Examples of coding sheets to record progress on emotional and belief understanding, and play are provided below, although teachers may also wish to devise their own forms.

EMOTIONAL UNDERSTANDING: RECORD FORMS

Levels of emotional understanding:

Level 1: Photographic facial recognition
Level 2: Schematic facial recognition
Level 3: Situation-based emotions
Level 4: Desire-based emotions
Level 5: Belief-based emotions

Instructions for administration

1. Start at Level 1 to establish the basal level = where child starts to fail.
2. To pass a level, the child must pass all 4 tasks.
3. To pass Levels 3–5, the child needs to answer correctly only the emotion questions, but the justification answers should be recorded.
4. Start teaching at the level the child fails any task.
6. Don't move up a level until the child has passed the previous one.
7. Be aware that a child might move "backward" between sessions, not only forward.

EMOTIONAL UNDERSTANDING: RECORD FORMS

Name of child: _____

Name of teacher: _____

Teaching day: _____ **Date:** _____

Level 1: Photographic facial recognition (✓ indicates a correct response and ✗ an incorrect response).

EMOTION FACE	RESPONSE	ADDITIONAL COMMENTS
HAPPY	☐	
SAD	☐	
ANGER	☐	
FEAR	☐	

EMOTIONAL UNDERSTANDING: RECORD FORMS

Name of child: _____

Name of teacher: _____

Teaching day: _____ **Date:** _____

Level 2: Schematic facial recognition (✓ indicates a correct response and ✗ an incorrect response).

EMOTION FACE	RESPONSE	ADDITIONAL COMMENTS
HAPPY	☐	
SAD	☐	
ANGER	☐	
FEAR	☐	

EMOTIONAL UNDERSTANDING: RECORD FORMS

Name of child: _____

Name of teacher: _____

Teaching day: _____ **Date:** _____

Level 3: Situation-based emotion (✓ indicates a correct response and ✗ an incorrect response).

STORY NO.	EMOTION SITUATION	RESPONSE	JUSTIFICATION
_____	HAPPY	☐	
_____	SAD	☐	
_____	ANGER	☐	
_____	FEAR	☐	

ADDITIONAL COMMENTS: _____

EMOTIONAL UNDERSTANDING: RECORD FORMS

Name of child: _____

Name of teacher: _____

Teaching day: _____ **Date:** _____

Level 4: Desire-based emotion (✓ indicates a correct response and ✗ an incorrect response).

STORY NO.	DESIRE	EMOTION OUTCOME	RESPONSE	JUSTIFICATION
☐	☐	HAPPY	☐	
☐	☐	SAD	☐	

ADDITIONAL COMMENTS: _____

EMOTIONAL UNDERSTANDING: RECORD FORMS

Name of child: _____

Name of teacher: _____

Teaching day: _____ **Date:** _____

Level 5: Belief-based emotion (✓ indicates a correct response and ✗ an incorrect response).

STORY	DES	BEL	EMOTION	RESPONSE AND JUSTIFICATION	EMOTION	RESPONSE AND JUSTIFICATION
☐	☐	☐	HAPPY	☐	HAPPY	☐
☐	☐	☐	SAD	☐	SAD	☐
☐	☐	☐	HAPPY	☐	SAD	☐
☐	☐	☐	SAD	☐	HAPPY	☐

ADDITIONAL COMMENTS: _____

BELIEF UNDERSTANDING: RECORD FORMS

Levels of belief understanding

Level 1: Simple perspective-taking
Level 2: Complex perspective taking
Level 3: Seeing leads to knowing
Level 4: True belief
Level 5: False belief

Instructions for administration

1. Start at the Level 1 and establish the basal level = where child starts to fail.
2. To pass a level, the child must pass all 3 tasks.
3. To pass Level 3, the child must correctly answer the knowledge question.
4. To pass Levels 4 and 5, the child must correctly answer the belief questions.
5. Start teaching at the level the child fails any task.
6. Don't move up a level until the child has passed the previous one.
7. Be aware that a child might move "backward" between sessions, not only forward.

BELIEF UNDERSTANDING: RECORD FORMS

Name of child: _____

Name of teacher: _____

Teaching day: _____ **Date:** _____

Level 2: Complex perspective-taking (✓ indicates a correct response and ✗ an incorrect response).

ITEM DETAILS	I SEE?	YOU SEE?	ADDITIONAL COMMENTS
1. _____	☐	☐	
2. _____	☐	☐	
3. _____	☐	☐	

BELIEF UNDERSTANDING: RECORD FORMS

Name of child: _____

Name of teacher: _____

Teaching day: _____ **Date:** _____

Level 1: Simple perspective-taking (✓ indicates a correct response and ✗ an incorrect response).

ITEM DETAILS	I SEE?	YOU SEE?	ADDITIONAL COMMENTS
1. _____	☐	☐	
2. _____	☐	☐	
3. _____	☐	☐	

BELIEF UNDERSTANDING: RECORD FORMS

Name of child: _____

Name of teacher: _____

Teaching day: _____   **Date:** _____

Level 3: Seeing leads to knowing (✓ indicates a correct response and ✗ an incorrect response).

ITEM DETAILS	SELF JUDGEMENT	JUSTIFICATION
SELF KNOW		
1 _____ ☐.		
SELF NOT KNOW		
2. _____ ☐.		

ITEM DETAILS	OTHER JUDGEMENT	JUSTIFICATION
OTHER KNOW		
1. _____ ☐.		
OTHER NOT KNOW		
2. _____ ☐.		

ADDITIONAL COMMENTS

BELIEF UNDERSTANDING: RECORD FORMS

Name of child: _____

Name of teacher: _____

Teaching day: _____ **Date:** _____

Level 4: True belief (✓ indicates a correct response and ✗ an incorrect response).

ITEM DETAILS	BELIEF	ACTION	JUSTIFICATION
1._____	☐	☐	
2._____	☐	☐	
3._____	☐	☐	

ADDITIONAL COMMENTS

BELIEF UNDERSTANDING: RECORD FORMS

Name of child: _____

Name of teacher: _____

Teaching day: _____ **Date:** _____

Level 5: False belief (✓ indicates a correct response and ✗ an incorrect response).

ITEM DETAILS	BELIEF AND JUSTIFICATION	ACTION AND JUSTIFICATION
UNEXPECTED TRANSFER (1)		
1._____	☐	☐
UNEXPECTED TRANSFER (2)		
2._____	☐	☐

ITEM DETAILS	BELIEF (SELF)	OTHER BELIEF	JUSTIFICATION
UNEXPECTED CONTENTS			
3._____	☐	☐	

ADDITIONAL COMMENTS:

PRETEND PLAY: RECORD FORM
Observe the child's *spontaneous play*, and code into:

Level 1: Sensorimotor play
Level 2: Functional pretence (two or fewer examples)
Level 3: Functional pretence (more than two examples)
Level 4: Pretend play (two or fewer examples)
Level 5: Pretend play (more than two examples)

Name of child: _____

Name of teacher: _____

Teaching day: _____ **Date:** _____

Level of spontaneous play: ☐

Description of spontaneous play activities:

Level of play reached with teaching: ☐

Description of play activities during teaching:

Additional Notes: